EXPORT MANAGEMENT

MODERN MANAGEMENT SERIES

Export Management

Edited by

M.K. Singh

Anant Mahadevan

DISCOVERY PUBLISHING HOUSE

NEW DELHI

First Published 1996
Reprinted-2010

ISBN 81-7141-084-7

Published by

Discovery Publishing House
4594/9, Darya Ganj
New Delhi-110002

Printed in India
at
Sachin Printers
Delhi

Preface

The phenomenal growth of commercial enterprises in the past decade or so has been the outcome of an equally remarkable spurt in surplus purchasing power, wage increase, liquidity of holdings and the advent of consumerism impelled by the remarkable technological development during the period. Enterprises and industrial conglomerates, trading services and hire-purchase firms alike have had to move fast to be equal to the opportunities provided by a growing national as well as international market. Industry and enterprises have had to change gears in a big way.

This collection of papers, articles, extracts and comments is concerned with the very practical aspects of effective export management. As such, it precludes theoretical and academic discussions. The writing on the wall in respect of the threatening balance-of-payments position of developing countries has been there for quite many years past, but so have been the signposts to better export management. The attempt of the editors is, therefore, to present the writings which together constitute a practical executive's (as well as students') handbook for improving his company's export performance. The least that the book can offer is, perhaps, the correct perspective on those aspects of export management which together constitute the anchor-point of modern export management in today's increasingly competitive international market-place. The subjects covered include export product development, official commercial representation abroad, export promotion, export market research and import management.

In our efforts we have been assisted in generous measure by our many colleagues and friends, professional managers and experts consultants. They would be too numerous to list—suffice it to say that without their guidance these papers and articles would not have been brought together into a cohesive whole. Nonetheless, we feel it our bounden duty to acknowledge the fruitful discussions we have had with Prof. P. Sarveshwar and Dr. Arun Nimbalkar of the Institute of Corporate and Industrial Management, Bombay; Dr. S. Ganesan of the Textile Managers Association, Aurangabad; Shri K. R. Wadhawan of the Centre for Research in Management Sciences, Manila, and Smt. Urvashi Palekar, Documentation Officer, Institute of Corporate Management, Faculty of Economics, University of Lagos, Nigeria.

Excellent computer and secretarial support services were provided by S/Shri Sameer Kak, Arvind Goswami and Raghuraj T. We are grateful to them.

We have attempted to minimise all printing errors, but hasten to add that we alone are responsible for those that still remain.

M. K. Singh
Anant Mahadevan

Introduction

Management may be defined as the process of efficient functioning based on correct choices and actions. However, in the modern world which is increasingly dependant on large organisations, the most significant situations are those which require organisational management. This implies decision and action in a context which is characterised by organised group or collective activity and the goals or objectives towards which the group effort is directed.

These objectives are pursued by managers, who make decisions pertaining to the desired objectives and concerning relationships among resources—the people, money and machines, materials and methods which can be effectively deployed to attain those objectives. Managers then see that their decisions are carried out and that they have the desired effect. When necessary, they use *control actions* to redirect their resources toward the desired objectives. Since managers of large organisations cannot literally to each and every thing that is required as a result of the decisions that are made, organisational management is a process of *working through others* to achieve broad organisational objectives, such as profit or social welfare, or specific objectives such as the development of a new product with success potential of the efficient and time-bound construction of a power plant.

Management may thus be thought of as involving two major elements, *planning* and *control* These two aspects of management apply to all areas of organised activity, such as the modern large firm represents. Planning involves decisions and actions concerning the future of the organisation. What type of business should be taken up? What kinds of manpower mix will be needed for effective functioning in the 1990s? What impact will increased leisure time have on the utilisation of the contemplated products?

Control involves decisions and actions related to the present organisations. How should production be scheduled to optimise machine-utilisation time? What should be the efficient allocation of workload among various levels of manpower? What mix of newspaper-radio-TV advertising would be best suited to the products?

Every manager is involved to some degree in both planning and control, but the jobs of many managers emphasise the control component. This is, in fact, true of many jobs which have the word 'planning' in their designation. The job of a production planning manager, for instance, is largely control oriented as it stresses the present and the immediate future rather than the long-term future—which is an intrinsic aspect of correct planning.

A number of developing countries stand on the threshold of rapid industrial development. If this development is to be successful in achieving domestic and export acceptance of their products, quality, price and delivery must be placed in proper perspective and continually improved. Management personnel in government departments; private industry; management, professional and trade associations; academic institutions; and so on must develop a genuine and growing interest in the use of quality control and all its facets to achieve these results. Awareness of the importance of quality, the specifications of desired and aimed-at quality, and planning for quality are essential decision and actions for governments and industrial and commercial enterprises—whether small or large.

Establishing a quality control system is hardly an alternative —it is becoming a necessity for the economic and social well-being for any country.

Quality control programmes and applications have grown rapidly in developing countries over the past decade with considerable promotion by various international organizations and numerous bilateral programmes, but also in no small measure by the inspiration of the phenomenal Japanese industrial and economic success, coupled with no reluctance on their part to credit much of their progress to the establishment of a quality control consciousness and to the application of such consciousness to the market.

It has been observed that several critical aspects of export marketing management are often overlooked in designing the overall export strategy. This lacuna is observed not only in export firms and organisations but also at the national level. India has been suffering increasing decline in its export performance, and this is due not only to the increasing competitiveness of the international market-palace. The common and most-often voiced complaint against India's exports is the lack of quality in its export commodities. This criticism applies especially to the non-traditional export commodities which hold the real promise of solving the difficult balance-of-payments position. Quality-consciousness is therefore of the utmost, even dominating importance.

On a national level there are quality control societies; other professional and trade associations; local' regional, and national seminars and conferences; training programmes and certification of practioners, university degree programmes; publications and literature promotion; product liability legislation and government compulsions for quality and safety; standardization; certification and quality marks programmes; export inspection programmes; legal metrology and related matters.

Measures to be taken: Much has been written on quality control in developing countries. It all makes reference, at least in part, to the following recommendations for developing an affective quality control programme at the national level:

1. Establish strong national leadership and a national plan, as through one or more influential national organizations, such as the national standards body, association of manufactures, management associations, engineering and other professional societies, universities and so forth. This implies the formation of a group or groups to spearhead the quality movement. This need not be a quality control society, *per se*, but should be a group that is well organized, influential and active. Develop a quality consciousness and concern for quality in key governmental, industrial, commercial, financial and academic leaders. This may be done by arranging for internationally known experts to conduct seminars for such leaders to emphasize the importance of quality in a developing economy—perhaps using the success of another country.

In the national plan give serious consideration to the establishment of reasonable trade policies to encourage competition and quality improvement, while promoting local manufacturers. Promote exports, and the necessity for local manufactures to meet international quality levels and standards.

2. Establish and actively support and publicize a national standardization effort. The adjunct of a quality certification programme with a publicized and recognized quality mark backed up by a sound programme of initial factory inspections, product testing, surveillance inspections and testing, and so forth is highly desirable. The development of a national capability in legal and industrial metrology and calibration is a necessary programme to support the certification efforts and industrialization in general.

3. Create government and commercial compulsion for reasonable levels of quality via quality requirements in purchase contracts, building specifications, standardization and certification, export inspection programmes and so on. Some quality requirements need enforcement from an organization or programme with a broader perspective than the manufacturer

himself or his immediate customer. (For example, the higher cost of electricity or even the cost of a fire from poor-quality electrical cable is most often not borne by the manufacturer of the cable or by the construction contractor. Without some independent enforcement of such quality, they may be tempted to cut their individual costs by supplying a low-grade cable). There are at least two levels of compulsion which may be created. One can be referred to asa "subtle compulsion" obtained by the political-technical activity of convincing responsible authorities to specify or require quality in products and services. The other may be referred to as "hard-core compulsion" obtained by the politico-technical-legal activity of decreeing by law that imported and/or manufactured products must conform to a given standard, with associated liabilities. Each of these forms of compulsion has its place in a national quality control system. Priorities based on national development, economy and public safety must be established. Programmes of enforcement, compatible with the requirements and scope of compulsion, must be created and supported to make the entire effort effective.

4. Establish media for exchange. Promote industrial applications. Hold seminars and publish transactions and journals. Develop training mannuals, texts, standards and so on. Develop study groups to study applications in other countries. Request and implement local projects funded by outside assistance. Direct these projects in accordance with the national plan. Develop local practitioners, lecturers, teachers and so forth for more intensive training.

5. Establish an extensive programme of training. This can be organized and spear-headed by the quality control society and/or other organization such as management associations, industry associations, governments and the like, especially for managers and practitioners. Academic institutions should be stimulated to develop courses for inclusion in key curriculla. In-company training should be encouraged and assisted.

The papers in the present compilation are intended as a handbook for a basic understanding of export management in today's highly complex, competitive and international industrial and commercial market place. As such, they will, it is hoped, be useful not only to the export executive but also students and scholars of management courses.

Contents

1

PRODUCT SUITABILITY AND PACKAGING FOR EXPORT

I

DETERMINING PRODUCT SUITABILITY*

With the exception of commodities for which rigid standards of quality and packaging are set, an exporter rarely finds that his product "as made" fits exactly the requirements of his selected target markets. Usually he will have to redesign or adapt his product or its packaging before he can export it successfully. The need for research into demand, types of products acceptable, and appropiate presentation and packaging becomes even more important when the product is a non-traditional export.

An exporter should find out if the trade is willing to sell his product and under what conditions. Sometimes exporters argue that a check on the acceptability of a product takes time, delays

*James J. ward is Bank of Ireland Professor Marketing at University College, Galway, in Ireland and a consultant on marketing training. This article is adapted from material appearing in *Export Marketing Management*, one of a series of ITC training guidebooks.

sales, costs money and may alert a competitor of the exporter's intentions. Yet the risks of not making a thorough check before committing major financial resources to developing a market are great. They include wasting time in false starts, wasting money on shipping the wrong types of product to the market, and losing the goodwill of importers, wholesalers and retailers. Exporters should assess the suitability and acceptability of their products before launching them on new markets.

The Basic Questions

For most exporters in developing countries, product problems are concerned with these principal questions:

1. Can the product or products now, available be exported and successfully sold in the target export markets?

2. What changes are needed in the product's construction or composition, its function and its packaging so that it can be sold in the target export markets?

3. How can the required changes be made, and how can the acceptability of the modified product be tested?

4. What opportunities might exist for the exporter to sell the new product? How should be go about finding these openings?

A manufacturer in a developing country is rarely in a position to make new product development the sole or decisive element in his export activities. He usually has to work within strict financial, organizational and manpower limitations all of which severely limit his ability to introduce new products. This does not mean that new product development is a luxury beyond his reach, but rather that it cannot and should not be the main force in his efforts to penetrate new markets. There is a place for new product development in his overall marketing plan, provided he has been able to find export markets for his existing products. Successfully exporting existing iterms generates the revenue, experience and expertise he needs to launch new products.

A further problem related to the export product that tends to be overlooked, but that is often decisive in the long run, is "product updating" or "product maintenance." There is no guarantee that a product, once developed launched and introduced, will continue to be successful, profit able export. Steps should be taken to review the product periodically and upgrade it, its packaging and its promotion if necessary. Successful companies have a product review at least once a year to ensure that the right measures are taken as regards product ingredients and design, packaging and presentation, and promotion. This extends the "life cycle" of the product and paves the way for a move to a new "product generation."

Export Suitability Investigation

The risks of not marking a thorough check on a product's acceptability are great. Whether a product is suitable for export depends basically on the answers to two questions:

1. Will the trade in the export market (importers, wholesalers, retailers) be willing to handle the product?

2. Will the consumers or end-users of the product buy it?

The methods for checking the export suitability of a product range from rudimentary, quick and inexpensive techniques to quite elaborate costly and time consuming procedures. It is up to the exporter, together with his agent or distributor, to decide on the extent of the investigation to be undertaken in each case.

Usually, it is advisable to lay down a checking procedure that (1) yields information on the product's suitability at different stages of the distribution process, *i.e.*, at the level of importers, wholesalers and retailers; (2) progresses, from simple, inexpensive techniques to more complex ones with a suitable "stop/go" control at the end of each; (3) includes direct consumer exposure (whether in simple or complex form).

As a rule, a three-step investigation is employed:

1. Study the product in relation to competitive products on the market.

2. Investigate trade acceptance of the product.

3. Test the product with consumers and endusers.

Conducting the product investigation programme in this order has a number of advantages. If the study of competing products is undertaken early, the exporter is already armed with the necessary background when he contacts importers or distributors, and he will be in a much better position to assess the information he receives from them. He will also very quickly see whether there is any justification in continuing his investigation, or whether he should abandon any further effort because his product is obviously not suited for the market, since it cannot compete with other products already being sold there.

Investigation of Competitive Products

The checklist presented here outlines the points to be looked into in a study of a product's competitveness vis-a-vis similar items already on the market. The product has to be examined in terms of its technical and quality characterstics, its packaging and presentation, the price structure for the item in the market in question and product services.

If this analysis shows that the product is potentially competitive with others already being sold on the market, the next step is to assess the trade's acceptance of the product. Updating the product is necessary to be certain that such aspects as design are appropriate.

Trade Acceptance Investigation

The aim of this second step in the export suitability study is to find out whether the trade will be able and willing to sell the product and under what conditions.

The exporter should first discuss the product with potential importers whose knowledge of the market and experience in selling similar products can provide an indication of whether adaptations or changes will be needed in the product and how important or urgent these are.

The exporter should next interview a representative group of wholesalers and retailers on the suitability of the product. This will give him a broader knowledge on which to base his decisions. It may also result in some consumers' or users' reactions to the product.

Several aspects need to be covered in this stage of the investigation. The packaging of the product, including handling instructions, must be such that products arrive at their destinations in a saleable condition. Faulty packing and non-observance of specifications for refrigeration, stacking and so on often make a product practically unsaleable by the time it arrives in the market.

The required sizes and dimensions of the product; the type of outer container in which it should be packed; the product's suitability for warehouse handling; how it should be stored or possibly refrigerated; what its price should be and what margin should be accorded to each participant in the distribution process are all important aspects that need to be studied.

Consumer and User Reactions and Acceptance

In general, consumer testing means choosing a representative panel of consumers, having them use the product and then asking them to record their impressions of it. This can be done in a number of ways. In single placement tests, the product is given to a group of selected consumers who are interviewed after the period of usage and requested to give their impressions and opintions on the product. A more elaborate formula involves comparative placement tests whereby the product to be introduced is given to consumers, together with a competitive product of a similar kind. In this case, too,

Steps in a Product Acceptability and Adaptation Exercise

Step	Action		Information needed		Results		evaluation and decision		
STEP 1	Determine the products suitability for export	→	Characteristics of the product, its packaging, services and price	→	Positive	→	Go to step 2		
				→	Negative	→	Correct deficiencies then go to step 2	→	Or abandon product
STEP 2	Assess the product's suitability vis-a-vis the trade	→	Trade acceptance check	→	Positive	→	Go to step 3		
				→	Negative	→	Correct problems, then go to step 3	→	Or abandon product

Step							
STEP 3	Determine to products acceptability to users and	→	Consumer acceptance check	→	Positive	→	Go to step 6
				→	Negative	→	Go to step 4 → Or abandon product
STEP 4	Decide on adaptation or redesigning required	→	—Specific adaptation of redesigning required —Cost and organization —Criteria and assessment —Plan of action	→	Feasible	→	Go to step 5
				→	Not feasible	→	Abandon product
STEP 5	Execute adaptation and redesign programme	→	Evaluation of results	→	Positive	→	Go to step 6
				→	Negative	→	Abandon product

(*Contd.*)

STEP 6

Draw up export marketing plan and proceed to export

consumers are interviewed, and their opinions and judgements on both products solicited.

Both methods have one disadvantage. They give information only on use and do not indicate whether the consumer would be prepared to purchase the product once it is put on sale. In order to get a clear idea of the consumer's willingness to buy, still more elaborate procedures should be used, such as test sales in small areas, for example in towns, or regional test markets.

At all stages of the acceptance checking sequence, it is vital for the various investigations to indicate not only the positive (or negative) reactions of the importer, the trade and the consumer, but also the reasons why the product is accepted or not, and what adaptations or improvements are needed in it or in its presentation.

Adapting the Product to the Market

An exporter rarely finds that his product "as made" fits the market requirements exactly Once the product's acceptability in the chosen market has been studied, using one or more of the above methods, the exporter may come to the conclusion that the present form of his product and the manner of its presentation are not suitable or acceptable for sale in the foreign market for a variety of reasons.

Action is needed to correct these deficiencies. including possible redesign of the product or its packaging.

A plan for product redesign or adaptation should include the following:

1. Design objectives: The changes and improvements needed in the product should be described in detail, as should modifications in its presentation and packaging.

2. Organization: Several managerial questions should be examined. Who is to take change of the adaptation programme?

Should outside experts be used? How will the exporter and the importer cooperate in this area?

3. Planning and budget: Time schedules and deadlines need to be set up, and the cost of the redesign programme should be decided upon. Similarly, a decision should be reached on how large an increase in the cost of the product itself would be acceptable as a result of redesigning and modifying it.

4. Execution: Actual adaptation can begin after all of the above have been solved. Drawings, models and prototypes should be made and reviewed in the light of the design aims. Some times the work can be carried out in stages, thus permitting progressive reviews while the modifications are under way.

5. Verification: A series of tests, again at the trade and consumer levels, should be carried out to ensure that the levels aim of all this actiivty a more suitable and acceptable product has been achieved. The reactions to the product should be tested among those who will be using the item.

Checklist for Studying Competing Products

I. Product

(a) Technical evaluation: raw materials used in competing products; their design; variety of models, types, sizes, shapes, colours available: previous changes, alterations and improvements in competing products; their adaptation to standards; origin of competing products (imported or local); their durability.

(b) Appraisal of quality: strength, efficiency, performance, appearance, suitability, ease of use of competing products.

(c) Legal protection: situation concerning patent rights and licenses of competing products.

II. Packaging and Presentation

(a) Technical evaluation: design, shape, materials used, closure of competing packaging; resistance to climatic conditions (heat; humidity and so on); ease and reliability of packing and packaging during shipping, handling, storage, display; compliance with official regulations.

(b) Attractiveness: size, shape, colour, convenience, quality impression, label design of competing packaging.

(c) Identification: shape, colour, label, trademark of competitors' packaging.

(d) Information conveyed on packaging product description ingredients, instructions for use.

III. Product Services

Types of service offered by competitive products—delivery installation, conditioning, parts and ac0essories, education in use, possibility of returned goods.

IV. Price Structure

(a) Consumer prices: basic list price; usual selling price; taxes (turnover, state or city); discounts (quality, cash payment); means of payment (cash, credit, installments): allowances for damaged goods; variations between regions and types of outlet.

(b) Price to the trade: range of prices; discounts; payment terms; allowances to importers, wholesalers and ratailers, by product, region, size of order, type of dealer.

II

EXPORT PACKAGING SPECIFICATIONS*

By using well defined specifications for their purchases of packaging, exporters should be able to get higher quality packages at lower costs. Obtaining the right type of packaging material at a reasonable cost is essential for profitable exporting.

*Johan Selin is ITC's Export Packaging Adviser.

The packaging material must be suited to the product being exported to the exporter's packing operations, the transport conditions on route to the foreign market and the overseas buyer's demands. Appropriate packaging specifications can help to assure that these requirements are met. They also provide an exporter with a sound basis for comparing offers from several different suppliers and can improve his bargaining position with the supplier he selects, for example in settling any eventual claims if the material delivered is defective.

Developing Specifications

Packaging specifications consist basically of an accurate, detailed description of the packaging supplies to be bought, whether these be readymade packages, material to be used in making packages or packaging accessories. On the basis of the information contained in the specifications, the packaging supplier is able to quote, manufacture and deliver the goods in accordance with the exporter's requirements.

Developing packaging specifications that are ideally suited to an exporter's product, his packing operation and his export market may take some time, perhaps even several years, as his packaging needs will become more precisely defined as he gains experience in selling abroad. (For this reason an exporter should not merely copy the packaging specifications used by others, a they may not be suitable for his export operation.)

An exporter's initial specifications, which are based on the information that he has on hand when he starts his export business, can be issued to the packaging supplier in the beginning "for guidance only." These first specifications should be preceded by preliminary discussions with one or more potential suppliers to avoid the inclusion of unnecessary or unrealistic details in the packaging specifications. such as materials that might not be available in the country. Discussions with the supplier selected should continue as subsequent orders are placed until the ideal specifications are arrived at, to the satisfaction of all parties. Obtaining packaging at a reasonable cost is essential for profitable exporting.

Basic Information Required

As a general rule, packaging specifications should contain at least the following information:

Type of package to be purchased (for instance, corrugated box or metal can).

Type of export product to be packed.

Characteristics of the export product, including the method of packing it, if relevant (for instance, for processed foods), and the requirements for protecting it during transport and distribution to the foreign buyer.

Mode of transport from the exporter to the overseas market.

Quantity and volume of the product to be packed in each unit.

Quantity of packaging required.

Grade and quality of the raw material to be used in the packaging, defined in measurable units, for instance, minimum strength according to a recognized test method.

Construction design of the package, illustrated by drawings if necessary.

Dimensions of the package, with realistic maximum and minimum tolerances in size.

Graphic design and detailed instructions for printing the revelent illustrations and texts on the package.

Special features or accessories of the package (for instance, closures, easy-opening devices, handles).

Type of box, wrapping, etc. in which the packaging material is to be supplied to the exporter.

Price of the packaging material.

Delivery schedule for the material.

Additional information could include:

Quantity tolerances for the packaging material ordered.

Classification of possible defects in the material and the degree to which such defects are admissible.

Applicable standard test methods of the packaging for quality control purposes.

Not all of this information can be considered as strictly part of technical specifications, as some of it may be relevant only at the purchasing stage, such as data on delivery time or price.

Each type of packaging material has its own particular requirements and therefore its own technical specifications. Some of the above-mentioned items of general relevance for most types of packaging are discussed in more detail below Initial specifications can be improved upon through discussion with the supplier.

Product Characteristics

Generally speaking, the more a packaging supplier knows about the product to be packaged, about the exporter's packaging operation and the distribution chain of the export operation, the better he will be able to supply effective and economical packages to the exporter.

In many cases, and especially for processed food products, it is important for the packaging supplier to know the exact characteristics of the product, such as its fat content, pH value, its nitrate content and other chemical components. Additional details, such as the temperatures under which the processed foods are packed, should also be specified. All of this information helps the supplier to select the right types of raw materials and packages.

Among details contained in packaging specifications in the type of package to be purchased. Examples of how such information could be stated in the specifications are given below:

> "Product X is highly hygroscopic and will cake if its moisture content exceeds 6 per cent by weight. It is packed at a maximum of 3 per cent moisture and the package must prevent pick-up of more than 3 per cent additional moisture over a period of one year under tropical conditions."

> "Product Y is filled at a temperature of 194°F (or 90°C) and is then rapidly cooled by immersion in water to room temperature."

> "The fruit is packed wet from the cleaning process, the cover immediately closed and the package placed in refrigerated storage of +41°F (+5°C)."

> "Product X is mildly acidic (pH value 5). contains anthocyanin, 50-70 mg NO_3 per kg of the product, approximately 3 per cent NaCl and can be considered as mildly corrosive."

Means of Transport

Background information on modes of transport and transport conditions is important for selecting packaging that will protect the goods being shipped against mechanical hazards. Such details are important for all types of products, whether they are perishable items or durable goods, and should be clearly stated in the specifications.

For example, the specifications might read: "The product is packed in the countryside and transported approximately 50 km by truck to the port, where it is loaded into inter-island schooners for transshipment to Canada by sea in unitized loads or freight containers."

Quantity to be Delivered

Ordering the optimum quantity of packaging is important for cost reasons. Standard items that a packaging supplier keeps in stock can be ordered in exact quantities because they are produced in large batches for many different clients. But for custom-made packages, a supplier has to arrange a special production run. which entails manufacturing an excess of the product to allow for waste, unacceptable quality and so on. It is therefore not possible for the supplier to gear his output to the exact order figures. The excess produced will in any case be included in the overall price that he charges the exporter for the packages. If an exporter orders a special custom-made package he should therefore allow for a certain variation in the quantity delivered. In his purchase order he should specify the tolerances he will accept above and below the quantity ordered. This is sometimes called "overage" or "underage."

Because the unit price of custom-made packages varies considerably depending on the quantity ordered (due to the set-up time of the machines before the supplier can start producing the packages), an exporter ordering custom-made packages should always ask for quotations on several different quantities to determine the most economical volume for his particular situation.

Packing for Delivery to the Buyer

The type of wrapping of other packing material used for shipping the packaging material to the exporter should be specified. With a little planning it might, for instance, be possible for an exporter to reuse the outer packing material that his new packages arrive in. A typical example of material that can be reused is corrugated boxes, which can sometimes be used for packing empty metal cans, glass and plastic bottles, or jars. Pallets can also usually be reused, as can inside cushioning material. Drawings should be included with the written specifications when it is necessary to indicate specific dimensions and tolerances for the packaging being ordered.

Price

Price is an essential element in specifications that are contained in a purchase order. In periods of rapidly rising prices, it may be difficult for a packaging supplier to give a fixed a price, particularly for orders with long delivery times and those placed on a yearly basis. Occasionally prices can be linked to fluctuations in recognized market prices, but this works only for increases (rather than decreases) in price and always in favour of the supplier. The best strategy for an exporter purchasing packaging is to negotiate fixed prices for long-term contracts—the increases in price will certainly come, but may be a little later than if a short-term ordering schedule is used. The main requirements are for the price clause in the order specifications to be stated explicitly and for the supplier to submit a written confirmation of the order.

Delivery Schedule

In principle, the delivery schedule for the total shipment or for partial shipment of the packaging should figure in the specifications, as well as in the supplier's confirmation of the order. For packaging materials purchased from suppliers in industrialized countries, particularly when large quantites are involved, the buyer sometimes includes a penalty clause in the specifications in case of delayed delivery. But a packaging supplier located in a developing country may himself have problems of delayed delivery of raw materials. In such a situation, it is difficult for the exporter to pin down the seller to a delivery guarantee. A sales contract for the import of packaging material stipulating payment by letter of credit (L/C) is one way to avoid this difficulty, although it is common practice for the buyer to extend the time of the L/C if the supplier so requests.

To simplify packaging specifications, various international codes have been drawn up on package design and construction. The codes can be used in specifications instead of written instructions.

For instance, for the package design shown at the top, the number "0200" can be given in the specifications rather than a written explanation.

The examples shown are from the International Fibreboard Case Code for corrugated and sold fibreboard boxes (for details, contact International Corrugated Case Association Secretariat, 37 rue d'Amsterdam, Paris 75008. France).

A similar code exists for folding cartons (for information: European Carton Makers Association, P.O.B. 408, Voorburg 2119. Netherlands).

Storage Requirements

Sometimes an order is delivered in several shipments on different dates, rather than together at one time. This may be the case, for example, if the exporter does not have the space to keep large stocks on his premises. The supplier may therefore agree to store part of the order in his own warehouse. The storage time involved and the eventual charges to be incurred by the purchaser of the materials, must be clearly stated in writing in the specifications—otherwise serious misunderstanding may occur later.

Tolerances

Suitable tolerances are an important aspect of realistic packaging specifications. One of the most difficult but, at the same time important questions in developing realistic packaging specifications is determining the minimum and maximum quality and quantity tolerance acceptable, both to the supplier and the exporters. Tolerances refer mainly to package dimensions to the grades of raw materials used in the packaing and to the quantities supplied.

For manual packaging operations, tolerances in the dimensions may not be important. But some sort of mechanical packing equipment in used, the exact tolerances required should be specified for the proper functioning of the packing machinery. The importance of dimensions tolerances also varies with the type of packaging. Such limits are much more significant for metal cans and glass bottle neck-threads, for instance than for corrugated boxes. For instance, for corrugated boxes a realistic tolerance for the dimensions is ± 5 mm. For glass bottles, on the other hand, a typical tolerance for the neck-thread in 0.5 mm or less at critical points. Dimensions tolerances should always be mentioned as + and —, either stated in the text of the specifications to marked on the eventual drawings attached to the specifications.

The determination of realistic tolerances can for close cooperation between the exporter and his packaging supplier. It is best to base initiate specifications on the general practice concerning tolerance levels and, if necessary, work towards stricter tolerances afterwards that are still acceptable to the supplier. The larger the production run, the easier it is for the supplier to adjust his machinery to the required precision level. Tolerances that are too narrow, even if they may be acceptable from a technical point, always result in a larger amount of off-standard rejects and waste in production and, consequently, a higher price for the packaging material.

Tolerances can also apply to the colours used in printing the packages or labels. The printed colour should match the sample initially given to the supplier and should be consistent throughout the entire batch of packages delivered. Numerical values of tolerances are not possible to establish without the use of sophisticated testing instruments, and therefore only a visual inspection can usually be made.

Classifying Defects

Most shipments of packaging material include a certain amount of defective material The specifications should therefore describe how the various types of defects are to be classified, what the basis is for rejecting or accepting any defective packaging material delivered, and how many defects can be allowed according to normal practice.

Defects in packaging material are usually classified in three categories with the following characteristics:

1. Class A—critical defects: The material cannot be used for its intended purpose under any circumstances.

2. Class B—major defects: The material deviates substantially from the specifications, but can be used for its original or for a secondary purpose with an extra effort by the exporter for example in added labour costs.

3. Class C—minor defects: The appearance of the package is slightly impaired, but, from a technical point, it is not defective.

The classification of defects into classes A, B and C depends to a great extent on the type of package and the exporter's packaging operations. Some examples of how delects are classified are given in the box at right.

Defects in Packaging Examples of Classification

Glass Bottles

Class A: Broken bottles; cracks in the bottle or neck finish; contaminated interior.

Class B: Glass weight below the minimum; dimensions for heigl t or diameter outside tolerances.

Class C: Uneven outer surface; slight off-colour glass substance; rough mould lines.

Metal Cans

Class A: Leaks in the body seam or at the manufactur's double seam; seaming compound missing; seriously dented flanges; missing or incomplete interior lacquering; contaminated interior.

Class B: Dents over 1 inch long; out-of-round shape; too much or too little seaming compound in the ends.

Class C: Dents less than 1 inch long; scratches on the ends of exterior surface of the body.

Labels

Class A: Wrong priniting; missing colour; labels stuck together; severe curl (machine labelling).

Class B: Rough-cut edges: poor print registration; colours off-standard,

Class C: Slight deviations in colour; slight curl.

Corrugated Boxes

Class A: Tears; punctures and holes; dimensions outside tolerance limits; cut-through liner at scores; non-compliance with box certificate stamp.

Class B: Excessive printing pressure; incomplete print; liners not adhering; off-square or open manufacturer's joint.

Class C: Blotchy printing; scratches; scuff marks or stains on the outer surface.

Polyethylene Bags

Class A: Holes; tears or gaps in side seals; odour; contamination.

Class B: Film gauge below minimum; foggy film; smeared printing.

Class C: Wrinkled bags; off-colour printing; rough-cut edges.

Reference to Test Methods

When quality control criteria, for instance for the materials used in producing the packaging, are mentioned in the specifications, they should include references to the standard test methods applicable for determining if the quality level is suitable. An exporter who buys packages only occasionally, in small quantities, will not be able to test all of his packages to control their quality. He should, of course, carry cut a simple visual inspection immediately after he receives the material, but a comprehensive quality control programme will usually be too complicated and costly for him on a regular basis. Knewing details about the product helps the supplier to furnish suitable packages.

Selected Package Testing Laboratories in Developing Countries and Areas

Brazil:	**Centro de Tecnologia de Embalagem de Alimentos (CETEA)** **Av, Brasil 2,880, CP 13100** **Campinas S.P.** **Instituto de Pesquisas Tecnologicas do Estado de Sao Paulo (IPT)** **CP 7141, 0100 Sao Paulo S.P.**
Hong Kong:	**Hong Kong Standards and Testing Centre** **Eldex Industrial Building** **12th Flaor, Unit A** **21A Mo Tau Wel Road** **Hunghom, Kowloon**
India:	**Indian Institute of Packaging (IIP)** **E-2 MIDC Area, Chakala** **Antheri (East), Bombay 400093**
Jamaica:	**Jamaica Bureau of Standards** **Packaging Centre** **8 Winchester Road** **Kingston 10**
Mexico:	**Laboratorios Nacionales de Fomento Industrial (LANFI)** **Av, Industria Militar No. 261** **Mexico 10, D.F.**
Morocco:	**Institut Marocain de l'Emballage et du Conditionnement (IMEC)** **Km 9,500 route de Nouasseur** **B.P. 8006** **Casablanca-Oasis**
Republic of Korea:	**Korea Design and Packaging Centre (KDPC)** **128-8 Yun-Kun-Dong** **P.O.B. 2325** **Chongro-ku, Seoul 110**

Thailand:	Thailand Institute of Scientific and Technological Research (TISTR) 196 Phahonyothin Road Bang Khen, Bangkok 10900
Trinidad and Tobago:	Caribbean Industrial Research Institute (CARIRI) Tunapuna Post Office Trinidad, W.I.

From time to time, therefore, he should send samples of his packaging to an independent laboratory that has the necessary equipment to perfrom the tests according to the standard procedures set down in the specifications. The nature of these tests can be outlined in the specifications.

Such laboratories can be found in all industrialized countries and in many developing countries. The list given below shows some such institutions in developing countries. Most package testing laboratories in developed countries belong to the International Association of Packaging Research Institutes (IAPRI). Further details on names and locations of such laboratories can be obtained from the IAPRI secretariat:

Mr. Frank Paine
Secretary General
IAPRI
Eyot Lodge
Petworth Road
Chiddingfold, Surrey GU8 4UA
United Kingdom

The quality control function in industrialized countries is sometimes handled exclusively by the supplier, and the full test data is transmitted to the buyer, who accepts the test results as his own. This, of course, is based upon complete confidence and collaboration between the buyer and the supplier. If such a procedure is to be used, it should be stated in the specifications.

The mere existence of packaging specifications should automatically lead to improvements in a supplier's own pre-shipment quality control and production supervision, especially if he knows that the material delivered will be inspected upon arrival and that samples will occasionally be sent to a testing institution for verification.

Claims

If a packaging supplier does not deliver according to the specifications, the exporter can make a claim against him for losses he has suffered. (A packaging supplier is liable only for the loss of or defects in the materials he has supplied, not for any indirect harm his packaging may have caused, for instance, damage to or loss of the product inside.) If an exporter has carefully drawn up his specifications, he will have a much better chance of getting reimbursement for packaging materials not supplied according to his requirements.

Maintaining Flexibility

Although an exporter should of course adhere to his foreign buyer's specifications concerning the type of packaging in which the export product is to be supplied, an exporter should not overlook the possibility of discussing the type of packaging if he runs into problems finding exactly the materials called for in the export order. As a matter of practice, buyers and sellers in industrialized countries discuss possible changes in the type of packaging to be used if the material specified turns out to be too expensive, for instance, or unavailable locally. Exporters in developing countries should not hesitate to discuss such problems with their overseas customers as well. Any cost savings that could be made in the packaging as a result could be shared with the overseas customer.

When printed packaging material is ordered, the printer must know exactly how the printed texts or diagrams are to be positioned on the material. For instance, in the case of plastic material supplied in rolls for packaging nuts, dried fruit or candy, at least eight different printing positions are possible, as shown on the satandard form above. The correct position can simply be circled, and the form can be attached to the specifications sent to the supplier.

2

SMALL BUSINESS IN EXPORT

I

OPPORTUNITIES FOR SMALL BUSINESS IN EXPORT TRADE*

Small business enterprises have an important role to play in a country's foreign trade. Governments should stimulate such firms to go into exporting. It is a widespread fallacy in many countries—especially in developing countries—to think that small business enterprises have little or no prospect of successfully selling in foreign markets. A study of the source of exports of countries as diverse as Japan, the United States and the Republic of Korea will reveal that small business enterprises have made a significant contribution to the growth of exports. For example, in Japan small enterprises in recent years have accounted for 30 per cent to 50 per cent of the total annual export earnings. In individual product sectors, the share of small enterprises in the total annual exports of each sector has

*Victor Santiapillai is Chairman of the Sri Lanka Emport Development Board, and was formerly Director of ITC. This article is reprinted from *Business Lanka*.

been even higher—60 per cent in the case of shoes and garments from the Republic of Korea, for instance.

The size of a company in itself does not exclude it from successfully exploiting foreign market opportunities. Many small enterprises export a greater proportion of their production than bigger companies, and exporting makes a major contribution to the profitability and viability of these enterprises. (For example, a recent survey carried out by the Small Business Administration of the U.S. Government shows that a number of member firms of a small manufacturers association had much greater export receipts in terms of gross sales than big companies with 250 or more employees.) In small countries with a limited population and a low purchasing power, the economic viability of even small units of production depends on a wider market base than the home market. Hence, however small an enterprise may be exporting can make a crucial difference to its profitability and to its ability to improve its business, by enabling it to absorb the costs of product adaptation, improvement of quality, and renovation and replacement of machinery and equipment.

Apart from their foreign exchange earning potential, small industries consciously designed as an arm of a government's national export development strategy can help achieve certain socio-economic objectives of economic development policy which large industry is not capable of realizing, Small businesses create employment opportunities spread out in many parts of a country and help contain the growth of unhealthy urban industrial centres. They offer potential for capital formation in the suburban and rural sectors and thus induce savings. They have also facilitated the development of new technical skills and appropriate technology suited to a country's environment.

Government in both developed and developing countries have therefore been adopting deliberate policies to develop enterprises to enable them to enter the field of international trade, thereby ensuring their survival and growth.

Why Small Firms Hesitate to Export

The misconception regarding the inability of small business to exploit market opportunities abroad is largely due to the fact that many developing countries such as Sri Lanka have gone through too long a period of import substitution oriented development in a comfortable protected home market. Consequently, the managements of small enterprises operating in this environment seem to suffer from a psychological barrier to venturing into unchartered foreign markets which they consider difficult and risky. The size of a firm does not exclude it from successfully exploiting foreign market opportunities.

In a number of other instances there is a genuine lack of knowledge ithin small business enterprises of market opportunities for their products in foreign markets. For example, a common misapprehension is that export orders are always big orders which small enterprises cannot cope with.

In yet other cases, lack of supporting export services and complicated export procedures and documentation at home have discouraged small business enterprises from turning to exports.

Such factors that inhibit the entry of small business concerns into international trade must be alleviated mainly through government policies and assistance measures.

Which Products Offer Potential

Small businesses have immense potential to contribute to the export trade and economic development of a country in a surprising variety of products, provided the product lines are carefully chosen on the basis of their techno-economic feasibility in relation to foreign market potential. It is essential therefore that entrepreneurs and managers in small businesses know, at least in broad terms, what types of products small enterprises have been selling successfully in the world market.

Products with unique features: Many small enterprises export a larger share of their production than larger companies. A common feature of most products which have been successfully sold in the world market by small enterprises is the uniqueness of the product in the target market. The basis of market planning and promotion on a small budget is the uniqueness of a finished product in terms of criteria such as quality, style, design, function or appeal to a special market segment. In the absence of some unique characteristic in his product which appeals to the buyer abroad, the small exporter joins the competitive rat race, in which he is likely to be left behind, because of the vast marketing and promotional resources at the disposal of the large companies. Further more, he could also find himself competing with local producers who are well established in their own markets. Small businesses have immense potential to contribute to the export trade of a country.

Unique products by definition are specialized in one form or another, such as in:

1. Function or purpose: for instance, watch parts, natural hair wigs, electronic components.
2. Style and design: such as high-value jewellery, antique reproduction furniture.
3. High quality: for example, hand knotted oriental carpets, hand-knitted jerseys, precision instruments.
4. Appeal to a unique market segment: for instance, one in which price is not a dominant factor, such as hand-sewn shoes and saddlery, or food items catering to the needs of an ethnic group within a country.
5. Distribution channels: such as items for giftware shops and gourmel food shops.

While the above examples are given for illustrative purposes. It is evident that the products mentioned lend themselves to classification under more than one unique characteristic.

It must also be noted that the products have been selected from the successful export experiences of small business concerns in the developing areas of the world.

Favourable production conditions: Another area in which small firms in developing countries have an advantage, because of favourable wages and other production conditions, is where price advantage is a key factor in the international market.

This is the case, for example, with garments, brushes and brooms, utility footwear and Christmas decorations, where the cost structures, especially of small enterprises in developing countries, are particularly favourable to long production runs at low unit prices. Furthermore, such items do not require sophisticated marketing techniques and costly promotional budgets, and consequently small enterprises will not have to bear heavy marketing costs.

An area in which small enterprises have had a very rewarding experience is the assembly of components, which is usually labour intensive. The multibillion-dollar market in costume jewellery or electronic gadgets comes readily to mind here.

Subcontracting of the assembly of components by producers in the developed countries to small enterprises in developing countries has been a technique increasingly adopted in this field. This has enabled small enterprises to achieve a high degree of participation in international trade.

In all these product sectors, small enterprises have a special advantage in that they can respond more quickly than larger companies to subtle changes in foreign market demand. Because of speedier decision marking in small concerns, they can be more flexible and quick in taking product adaptation measures and rescheduling deliveries to meet, say, unexpected changes in seasonal demand.

Measures to Encourage Small Exporters

The extent to which small enterprises will participate in the export trade of the country depends largely on the efficacy of the assistance and supporting services available to them from the government agencies or parastatal organizations entrusted with the task of marking small enterprises progressively export oriented.

For example, countries such as the United States. Japan, India and the Republic of Korea have developed over the years effective institutions and measures to activate and assist small businesses to participate in international trade. The results of this policy are clearly seen in the contribution of small enterprises to the export trade of these countries.

A brief review of the critical areas in which small enterprises need assistance to enter the field of international trade would, therefore be useful.

Industrial estates: In order to be effective. any national programme for the development of exports by small businesses must include both upstream elements bearing upon the development and supply of export products as well as downstream aspects relating to export marketing and promotion. Unless constraints in both areas are alleviated and active support is given to both product development and export marketing, small enterprises are not likely to become export oriented.

With this objective in mind, a number of countries have organized industrial estates or parks of various types for small enterprises that wish to export. These industrial estates provide a package of facilities which respond to the needs of small enterprises with respect to both upstream and downstream elements.

The grouping of small export industries in industrial estates is a means of achieving for them advantages such as:

1. Internal economies through common infrastructure facilities.

2. Complementary economies through promotion of inter firm relations and optimal utilization of common service facilities.
3. Aggregation of a sufficiently large number of small enterprises to meet big export orders, thus ensuring quality standards and delivery dates.
4. Economies in collecting and analyzing market information and providing maketing advice.
5. Facilitation of export documentation and procedures.
6. Facilitation of the provision and supervision of special credit arrangements for the benefit of small export enterprises.

This type of integrated approach to the development of small export enterprises has been highly effective.

Marketing information: In the absence of such an institutional base, the government should at least adopt measures to remove the main constraints faced by small enterprises in venturing into the export market where risks are great and profits are low during the initial development stage.

To begin with (bearing in mind that many small enterprises historically have been oriented to supplying the home market), these enterprises will have to be apprised of the type of products they could hope to develop for export, the alternative marketing channels open to them their competitive strengths and weaknesses, and a whole array of related market information. Most products successfully sold on the world market have some unique features. Unique products are specialized in one from or another, such as watch parts in terms of function.

This would enable them to make a decision about the products and target markets on which they should concentrate their export effort. This should be the responsibility of the national trade promotion agency or the institution responsible for small industry development.

Export financing: A key element in the development of supplies of a product for export is the availabilty as well as the cost of finance for expansion of small enterprises.

II

PAYMENT FOR EXPORTS: KEY CHECKS FOR A SMOOTH TRANSACTION*

If you are an exporter who is trading on the basis of payment for your goods under a documentary letter of credit, you need to comply exactly with strict requirements if the transaction is to proceed smoothly. Failure to do so may lead to delays in receiving your money or at worst your being unable to obtain payment at all. If you are to be paid for your exports when selling under a documentary letter of credit, you must ensure that your documents meet exacting requirements.

In order to overcome such problems, it is essential that terms of the letter of credit with which you can comply are agreed between your buyer and yourself at an early stage, preferably at the time that the sale is made. This will help to eliminate, as far as possible, later errors and the need for time-consuming re-negotiation. Additionally, documents called for in the letter of credit must be completed accurately and consistently, and submitted to your bank within the time limits stipulated in the credit.

Although you may assume that this is a simple operation, in practice the statistics show otherwise. For example, a recent study by the U.K.'s Simplification of International Trade Procedures Board (SITPRO) revealed that up to 60 per cent of sets of documents lodged with banks by exporters under documentary letters of credit in the United Kingdom were rejected

*By the Simplification of International Trade Procedures Board (SITPRO) helps U.K. exporters rationalize their international trade procedures and the documentation and information flows connected with them. SITPRO is the United Kingdom's national trade facilitation organization.

on first presentation because they were either incomplete or incorrect. A further analysis revealed that the majority of these rejections were due to minor mistakes or general carelessness.

The pattern is almost certainly similar in other countries.

The following checks and general guidance notes were drawn up by SITPRO through its Payments Procedures Working Group. The list cannot by nature cover every situation likely to arise with a documentary credit, but it could, if read and followed thoroughly, help you to overcome some of the problems that lead to delayed or even lost payment for your goods.

Key Checks

Documents must be accurate and consistent and presented to the bank within the time limit. Immediately on receipt of the letter of credit read and re-read it very carefully and check the terms against your contract of sale. It is fundamental to:

Check that the letter of credit is of the type that you and the buyer agreed, for example irrevocable and confirmed, irrevocable.

Check that its expiry date is sufficiently far ahead for your goods to be shipped and for you to obtain the required documents and present them to the bank in time.

Check that you can meet the terms and conditions in the letter of credit andc an obtain the required documents exactly as called for in the letter of credit.

Check that the spelling in the letter of credit is correct—you should take up any misspellings immediately with your buyer.

Ensure that if any amendment or extension is necessary you immediately ask your buyer to instruct the issuing bank accordingly; see that advice of amendment of the credit is received without delay.

Remember, the letter of credit is the bank's mandate to pay you for your shipment. The bank has no discretion: It is not allowed to approve errors and/or inconsistencies, of whatever nature and however small, in the export documents that you present to it and will not pay you in such circumstances.

When you ship the goods and present the bill of exchange (sometimes called a draft) if any—and documents under the letter of credit to the bank, ensure that:

You present these documents without delay, within the expiry date of the letter of credit and the specified period of time after the shipping documents have been issued.

You have met all the terms and conditions of the letter of credit, including the presentation of documents that *exactly* meet the stipulations of the letter of credit.

Your documents are complete and consistent with one another.

Detailed Checks

Check that details such as the date and place of shipment are correct in the documents. If you do not comply with the requirements, you may not be able to-receive payment from the bank. You should also carry out a number of specific checks on your export documents, in addition to the key checks listed above. The following are the most important.

. By what means is the letter of credit available?

Payment—either against documents, or against documents accompanied by a sight bill (draft) on the named paying bank.

Acceptance—against documents accompanied by a bill (draft) on a named bank payable at a certain time (sometimes called usuance or term), for example 30, 60 or 90 days after the date specified.

Negotiation—against documents accompanied by a sight bill (draft) or time (usuance or term) draft drawn on the issuing bank or buyer.

2. Is the letter of credit payable in your home country, the country of importation or a third country?
3. Is your name and address and that of your customer complete and spelled correctly?
4. Is the amount of the letter of credit correct, and is it issued in the agreed currency?
5. Is the letter of credit in accordance with the terms of your sales contract, for instance, "ex works," "free carrier," FAS, FOB, C&F, CIF or other terms expressed in your original offer or proforma invoice etc.?
6. Are the description quantity and weight of goods lis ed in the letter of credit in accordance with the terms of your sales contract?
7. If bills (drafts) are called for have they been drawn up as agreed, for instance, at sight, or at a stated time (usuance or term)? On whom are they to be drawn?
8. Do the shipping and expiry dates and the period of time for presentation of the shipping documents after their date of issuance allow you sufficient time for processing the order, effecting shipment and presenting the documents to the bank with which the letter of credit is available?
9. Is the correct type of shipping document called for? (Remember, transshipment must be allowed if your shipping document is a combined transport (multi-modal) shipping document).
10. Can you obtain insurance cover against the risks specified in your letter of credit? Does the letter of credit request an insurance policy or insurance certificate?

11. Do any of the documents require or preclude any special declarations, statements or endorsements?

12. Have you obtained any necessary import or export licenses?

13. Are partial shipments allowed?

14. Are the shipping details such as place and date of shipment, port of destination and so on correct? (With combined transport it is essential for your letter of credit not to specify ports of shipments/destination but merely places of taking in charge and delivery of your goods).

15. If your goods are of a type that might or will require on deck stowage; does the letter of credit stipulate "on deck shipment allowed"?

Presentation of Documents to the Bank

The bank has no discretion: It is not allowed to approve errors of whatever nature. When you present your export documents to the bank, you must make sure that:

You present the documents exactly as called for in the letter of credit.

Your documents are complete and correct in number, type and content.

Your documents are consistent with one another.

Your documents conform exactly to the stipulations in the letter of credit.

Your documents can be identified as relating to your goods by means of corresponding shipping marks and package numbers.

Your insurance documents are of the type called for and cover the risks specified in the letter of credit.

You present your documents to the bank as soon as possible. You must present them within the specified time after issuance of the shipping documents and within the validity of the letter of credit. Remember that you will not paid if there be are any discrepancies. Minor mistakes or carelessness are often the cause for a bank's rejection of documents.

Some Common Discrepancies

Your export documents might not be in order for a variety of reasons. You must remember that you have to act in accordance with the requirements of the letter of credit you have received.

A recent study carried out by several banks in the United Kingdom revealed that over 20 per cent of sets of documents that they rejected were not acceptable for one of the three following regional.

1. The letter of credit had expired when it was presented to the bank.
2. The documents were presented after the period stipulated in the letter of credit.
3. The shipment was late.

Other reasons that documents might not be acceptable to the bank are:

The shipping document is claused (unclean—"dirty").

A charter party bill of lading has been issued when it is not specifically authorized in the letter of credit.

There is no evidence that the goods have actually been "shipped on-board," when the letter of credit calls for on-board shipment.

Shipment is made between ports other than those stated in the letter of credit.

The goods are shipped on deck when this is not permitted under the letter of credit,

An insurance document of a type other than that required by the letter of credit is presented.

The insurance risks covered are not those specified in the letter of credit.

The insurance cover is expressed in a currency other than that of the letter of credit.

The shipment is under-insured.

The insurance is not effective from the date of shipment or dispatch.

The documents are inconsistent with each other.

The description for spelling of the goods on the invoice(s) differ from that in the letter of credit.

The weights of the goods differ between documents.

The amounts shown on the invoice(s) and bill of exchange (draft) differ.

The marks and numbers for the goods differ between documents.

The amount drawn is less than the amounts stipulated in the letter of credit (when part shipments are not permitted under the letter of credit).

The amount in the letter of credit is exceeded.

The bill of lading does not evidence whether freight is paid or not (conditional).

The shipment is short, *i.e.* less than the full amount of the order is shipped.

The documents called for in the letter of credit are absent.

The bill of exchange (draft) is drawn on a wrong party.

The bill of exchange (draft) is payable on an indeterminable date.

The bill of lading, insurance document or bill of exchange (draft) is not endorsed correctly.

The copy of the freight account is not attached (when called for by the letter of credit).

Signatures or witnessings, where required, on documents presented are absent.

The documents contain facsimile signatures, when these are not allowed.

If mistakes are made in your export documents and if the discrepancies cannot be corrected and the documents re-presented within the required time limits, you will lose your right to payment under the letter of credit. (It might in some instances be possible for you to correct discrepancies, but this would have to be done and the re-presentation would have to be made within the expiry of the letter of credit and with in the specified period of time after the date of issuance of the shipping document).

In some cases you may be able to persuade the bank to make payment to you against an in demnity in respect of the discrepancies. But this does not mean that you will automatically be entitled to receive payment. If your buyer refuses to approve the discrepancies, you will have to refund the money you have received, plus interest.

Sources of Further Information

The publication Guide to Documentary Credit Operations, issued by the International Chamber of Commerce (ICC), provides further information on documentary letters of credit and includes then "Uniform Customs and Practice for Documentary Credits," to which most letters of credit are subject. This publication can be obtained from ICC Services S.A.R.L., 38 Cours Albert Ier, F 75008 Paris, France.

Some banks also provide advisory booklets containing information on documentary letters of credit. These are usually available free of charge.

Some Hints for Export Sales Missions

Before embarking on an overseas sales mission, make sure that you have a working knowledge of documentary letters of credits, if this is the method by which you wish to secure payment for your exports. Also consult the shipping department of your company to obtain expert advice on any particular requirements in the country you are visiting and the financial department to check the credit-worthiness of potential customers.

If possible at the time of sale and when negotiating terms of the letter of credit, try to make sure that you obtain a name and telephone number at your buyer's firm with whom any queries on the requirements of the letter of credit can be taken up personally on receipt of the credit in your shipping department. This could save much time.

Many types of financing schemes appropriate to the particular needs of small enterprises in a given country have been devised over the years in both developed and developing countries. These schemes have certain common features. First, finance is made available on the basis of the viability of the export project, rather than on the credit-worthiness of the enterprise. Second their is a grant element in the provision of finance for expansion of fixed capital to help the enterprise over the hump of initial development costs. Third, medium and long term, as well as short-term, loan finance is available at concessional rates of interest. Fourth, easy terms with respect to the amortization of capital and payment of interest are provided.

Help with export formalities: Other critical areas where a new small exporter needs a helping hand are terms of sales arrangements with the foreign buyer or collaborator, and export documentation required in both the exporting and importing country.

The small enterprise has little experience in negotiating with foreign enterprises the terms of international subcontracting arrangements, sales contracts and other forms of collaboration in marketing. Likewise there is a bewildering maze of export control; exchange control; and port, customs and shipping documents that have become so complex that proper compliance with the requirements is a problem for the new exporter.

The assistance of a national trade promotion agency or specialized service institutions can be most useful here.

Role of export houses: Expost houses and trading companies have played a very useful role in developing the exports of small enterprises by providing them with information needed for product adaptation; by being responsible for farming out large orders to a number of small enterprises; by holding themselves responsible for delivery and quality; and generally taking care of export financing, export marketing, and transport and insurance arrangements, as well as after-sales servicing of export orders.

The export marketing problem of the small enterprises could be taken over by specialized export marketing entities as has been demonstrated in a number of developed as well as developing countries. This will leave the small enterprises free to concentrate on the development of the product and its supply aspects.

3

EXPORT-ORIENTED FINANCIAL INSTITUTIONS

David Gordon*

Financial institutions, especially commercial banks and development finance companies, can provide key services to the export community. Export financing and export financial services are among the key elements in an effective national trade promotion framework in an developing country. Because of their important role in the national trade expansion programme, financial institutions in these countries should assure that their operations are geared to the needs of the foreign trade sector. By regularly reviewing their practices and procedures, such bodies can determine what new methods and programmes should be adopted to best serve the country's exporters, given the often rapidly changing international trading environment.

Among the various types of financial institutions that exist in developing countries, the ones that are the most important

**David Gordon* is a former Director of the World Bank in Washington, D.C., USA. This article is based on a contribution by Mr. Gordon in a new ITC handbook. *The Financing of Exports from Developing Countries*.

for the financing of exports are the relatively long-established commercial banks and the more recently created development finance companies (DFCs) and export banks.

This article broadly reviews the kinds of financial facilities and assistance that these entities can provide to the export sector and explains the principal techniques they can use to carry out this task.

Types and Sources of Export Financing

The different types of credit facilities that DFCs, export banks and commercial banks provide for the purpose of export financing in many countries are summarized below:

1. Long-term investment loans: These are provided principally through DFCs, but also increasingly through commercial or mixed banks, to finance part (often the foreign exchange portion) of the capital requirements of projects that conform to government policy and priorities, among which export projects usually rank high.

2. Export production loans: These are generally made by commercial banks, but by DFCs as well, on a short-term basis, and in local currency, to finance working capital needs of all kinds.

3. Export credits: These are provided by the commercial banking system or by special export banks to finance the goods from the time of sale unlil payment is received, period that may range from a matter of days to several years, depending on the nature of the goods and the international competitive situation.

4. Export credit guarantees: These usually do not involve funds in themselves but are rather an undertaking by a government agency to protect the export-financing bank against loss on the transaction. The credit programmes are man-dated and largely supported by national goverments. The necessary financial resources are provided to the intermediary banks

through budgetary advances and central bank rediscounting at low interest rates, and are passed on at below-market rates to export firms that meet the eligibility criteria. Moreover, these firms usually have preferred, and sometimes automatic, access to the often limited loan funds. (Such credit advantages are among the most powerful aids and incentives to export efforts. No country can afford not to make use of them, since almost all of its competitors do so).

The listing above suggests a rather neat demarcation between credit categories and a clear division of labour among the financial institutions involved. In actual fact, there is a good deal of variation on these two points from country to country, reflecting different and changing traditions and laws. Often institutional roles overlap considerably, and in several countries universal banking—where all the principal functions of financial intermediaries are performed within a single institution—is strongly favoured.

In almost all countries there is joint financing of major projects, reflecting the differing types of funding required for the various stages and purposes ("bridging" versus permanent commitments, foreign exchange versus local currency, investment versus working capital), for which the resources of one institution or the other are respectively better suited. The use of joint financing also reflects the common desire to be associated with projects of high priority and prestige and to minimize the risks of such operations through sharing.

The financial community in almost every country thus forms a close network based on informal consultation and collaboration, apart from its links stemming from normal financial transactions. Export financiers are even more closely knit than those in other segments of the financial sector. The discussion that follows of export financing functions and the institutional units through which they are performed needs to be placed in that context.

Development Finance Companies

In most countries the DFCs were originally conceived as the leading agents of the nation's developmental thrust. Typical mandates envisaged for them included seeking out and setting up worthly projects; mobilizing and allocating investment resources; helping to diversify financial instrumentalities and to upgrade business accounting and management standards; and generally being a laboratory, an example and a source of initiative to foster a healthy, broadly-based capital market. Although they have not always fully lived up to such hopes, they have fairly consistently been effective allocators of resources, both domestic and foreign. Furthermore, they have improved standards of project appraisal and management and have very usefully played both a promotional and an advisory role in diverse circumstances.

As a rule, the development of export production was not a primary concern of the early DFCs. Rather, in line with prevalent opinion and policies at the time, the project proposals they received and approved were mainly for import-substitution industries, although some involved the processing of domestic raw materials for export. With the growing government attention to and incentives for export promotion, evident in some countries from the mid-1960s, the emphasis of the DFCs in those countries shifted correspondingly, and a number of them soon moved to the vanguard of the national export drive.

Some of the principal operational differences between administering export-oriented and import-substitution loan projects are discussed below.

1. Project appraisal: The criteria and methods for reviewing export (or export-equivalent, that is foreign-exchange-earning) projects would, in most respects, resemble those applicable to import-substitution industries. (These are discussed at length in the literature on project evaluation, and in the manuals of individual DFCs, and will not be repeated here.) The qualities

to be expected and sought in suitable sponsors for the two types of projects would often be somewhat different. For export projects a more outward-looking, perhaps adventurous attitude would be needed in the sponsor, as well as familiarity with foreign market conditions and contacts. Otherwise, however, the appraisal standards and procedures would differ from those for import-substitution projects mainly as to detail (for instance, certain types of information needed) or emphasis.

2. Foreign exchange consequences: An analysis of the foreign exchange effects should be an important part of the appraisal for either an import-substitution or an export (or export-equivalent) project. For this purpose it is not adequate merely to balance off the direct foreign exchange cost of production inputs against the value of the export goods produced or the imports to be replaced. For one thing, the prices of both export and imported goods in the domestic market may be distorted by a number of factors. A potentially favourable flow of foreign exchange income may in some cases thus exact an unduly high price in national currency expenditure. In certain circumstances it may be found that; for a proposed export project, the resources required for the manufacturing or processing activity in question might be used more advantageously elsewhere in the national economy. (The costs and benefits of projects in terms of foreign exchange can be measured by various formulae).

3. Markets, technology and quality: The financial community in most countries forms a close network based on informal consultation. Markets for export industries are likely to differ considerably from those for import-substitution enterprises. The latter can be reasonably approximated by import statistics and trends and by domestic sales. The international market from the standpoint of most developing country producers, offers many opportunities but may also be hazardous, with strong and efficient competitors lying in wait. Moreover, the market is not homogeneous. In many product lines, for example, garments, leather goods, electronics and machinery, it is

highly segmented and constantly shifting with changes in style or technology. Moreover, different suppliers around the world are always striving to part their costs or to gain some other marginal advantage. Inevitably, too, standards of technology, style and finish are more demanding for sales abroad, where a wide variety of optional sources is available, than in the protected home environment.

The purpose of these observations is not to discourage businessmen from undertaking export ventures, or DFCs from assisting them, but rather to stress the need for both parties to do so with their eyes open and to make adequate preparations. Nor is it intended to suggest that every export initiative involves a similar degree of complexity and risk. (Japan first became a major force in world markets with textiles and inexpensive metal and mechanical goods, and the Republic of Korea with textile products, wigs and plywood. Both countries moved progressively into higher technology items).

One of the purposes served by a DFC's appraisal of export projects, and by the advice it gives to its clients, should be to check whether the special risk and requirements of projects for particular categories of goods have been given due attention. The DFC itself will not normally have the necessary expertise to recommend how all potential problems should be dealt with. Its appraisal staff should, however, possess a good perception of the kinds of questions that need to be asked, some knowledge of how to look for answers, and a capacity for independent judgement as to the consistency and comprehensiveness of the answers provided.

For specific technological and marketing guidance involving more complex considerations than for domestically oriented projects, the DFC could presumably look, among others, to:

(a) The project sponsors themselves and their technical staff or consultants, including representatives of a proposed foreign partner firm, if any. These would, of course, not be wholly disinterested experts. They would have a stake in the appraisal's conclusion being favourable, although the real interest of a foreign partner might not always be identical with that of the domestic company. But they would be the best informed about the sponsors' intentions and expectations and should bear the main burden of project justification.

(b) Official agencies concerned with economic planning, industry, trade policy, exchange control, science and technology, in order to ascertain how the project would accord with the national plan priorities, what tax or other benefits it could expect and whether foreign exchange for the current requirements of its operations could be reasonably assured, as well as to obtain leads to other relevant sources of information.

(c) National universities, engineering schools to consulting firms.

(d) International technological reference services of data banks, for instance those organized by international organizations, by some major research institutes and by certain private firms. These sources could probably be pinpointed by the national technology office or engineering university.

(e) A highly qualified independent foreign consultant.

Thus, although a DFC would seldom be qualified to speak authoritatively on most of the technical and marketing questions that require examination for an export project. It could still occupy a central place in the information-gathering and review process outlined above, as a catalyst and key controller of that process, because of its authority, in most cases, to decide whether or not to finance a particular project.

4. Reorientation of existing industries: Given the bias toward import substitution and projection of the domestic market that prevailed in most developing countries during the early development decades, much of their existing industrial

structure is ill-suited to make even cautious ventures into exporting. A few subsectors, such as handicrafts, garments, wood, leather and rubber products, involve simple technologies, little investment and relatively high labour content, and so enjoy a comparative advantage over the products of developed countries and even of the "first-generation" newly industrializing countries (NICs).

The major industrial installations, on the other hand, which have absorbed large amounts of the country's scarce investment capital and of its technical and managerial talent, may too often remain high in cost, with underutilized capacity. They may be in danger of obsolescence before they ever really function as was intended. In some cases, at least, such plants might be brought up to reasonable standards of productive efficiency and, incidntally, could begin to earn their own way in terms of foreign exchange by orienting them in part to the export market. To do this would require measures much move far-reaching than relatively short-term export incentives.

Some DFCs should be able, and be expected, to take a leading role in such a targeted industrial reorientation effort. For instance, they may be well placed to:

(a) Identify industries and individual plants that are currently in economic trouble, but that have potential for export sales if strong initiatives are taken to improve production, management of their financial structure.

(b) Enlist the talent needed to diagnose these industries' specific ills and to prescribe and eventually carry out appropriate remedial programmes for them.

(c) Establish, in cooperation with other institutions and government agencies, the necessary financing package and supporting measures for individual firms, to be conditioned on specified and attainable improvements in production and export performance.

(d) Provide, as part of this package, resources (loan or equity funds, as may be appropriate and prudent) to restructure the firm's obligations, restore its solvency and enable it to fulfill the specified conditions.

(e) Continue to act as a counsellor to the firm and to monitor its progress during the period of adjustment and recovery.

In the performance of this role, the DFC would clearly have to cooperative very closely with the national government and with the international lender(s) concerned, as well as with other domestic financial institutions.

5. Loan supervision: Systematic follow-up is no less essential for DFC-financed export projects than for those serving the home market. But export projects would be more complicated and less capable of fitting a procedural routine than domestic-oriented projects. For example, supervision of export projects would involve taking account of the effects of export incentives and determining whether the client uses them to maximum advantage; of assessing international market trends for the project's product line, perhaps even of new opportunities that could be exploited by changing that line; of determining the reliability of the product's major foreign buyers, the safety of credit terms extended to them, and the chances and likely time span for recovery of any losses from a credit guarantee fund; and so on.

While DFCs would be able to examine directly the premises, production operations and inventories of export borrowers, they could not normally follow their clients' sales (or check on their customers) abroad, as they might in the domestic market. Information on these aspects of the borrower's operations could be obtained only indirectly, through shipping and payment documents and commercial reports. Much of the documentation would be generated and handled by commercial banks providing short-term working capital and export credits. Close working relations with these banks would be essential.

Export promotion and information services maintained by the government, if any, through its embassies abroad or separately, might also be used, for example, to check on the situation of important delinquent customers.

Exporters should be held to essentially the same standards for the fulfillment of their obligations as are borrowers for domestic projects. The tax concessions and other incentives they receive are intended to compensate for their additional costs and risks, and a DFC should not be expected to subsidize them additionally. However, in proceeding against arrears or collateral security, the DFC must take account of the special circumstances of the export business and seek constructively to adjust debt service obligations when necessary to enable a borrower to recover from temporary difficulties.

Possible Operational Problems for Export Projects

It is in the nature of development banking that its operations seldom follow a routine, repetitive pattern. DFCs are expected to be imaginative and broadly competent in problem-solving and able to deal with the unpredictable. Naturally the unpredictable is more likely to occur after approval of the loan for a project. The uncertainties increase as the products concerned move into export markets.

The paragraphs below outline some of the difficulties that might arise in the course of a DFC's follow-up work on export projects. They are not meant to be representative but merely illustrative examples.

Cost overrun: This occurs when the total financing provided to construct and equip the project is clearly not going to be sufficient to complete it as planned (this may happen in the execution of any kind of project, whether for domestic or export production, and has been especially common in the past inflationary decade). If this situation is not quickly dealt with, the project could be jeopardized or seriously delayed, with major loss to the sponsors and to the national economy. The

DFC itself would not normally be faced with an immediate financial risk, since at that stage it would probably still have adequate collateral security. But it would nevertheless have a good deal at stake as the project's main institutional backer. It should, therefore, move as quickly as possible to:

1. Establish, in concert with the project sponsors, auditors, engineers, contractors and others having information, the amount of the likely cost overrun and its foreign and local currency components.

2. Ascertain (employing independent experts if necessary) the reasons for the overrun, and in so far as possible determine responsibility for it.

3. Investigate whether cost savings (for example, by changes in capacity or design) might reduce the overrum without disproportionate harm to the project.

4. Negotiate with the sponsors, contractors and others concerned, and consult with the legal and financial authorities (including probably the DFC's own ultimate financial source), to decide on and pursue a course of action for remedying the overrun. This might entail legal action, financial contributions by sponsors and possibly the contractors, supplementary financing from the DFC and perhaps other lenders (foreign or local) or, if completion of the project seems unfeasible, liquidating the project with minimum damage.

5. Make appropriate adjustments to the project loan agreements, re-payment schedules and financial projections, reflecting the decisions taken in step four above.

This is, of course, a greatly simplified sketch of the set of problems—different each time—posed by substantial cost overrun and the responses that a DFC may be called upon to make.

Deficiency in operating funds: A company might be faced, at any time after it starts operations, with a shortage of funds for its current needs. Normally these would be met routinely from current revenues or short-term borrowings. But extended periods of depressed demand, a sharp rise in costs relative to sales prices or other exceptional circumstances might impose a squeeze on both the cash position and creditworthiness with the banks. If foreign exchange is needed in more than normal amounts, for instance for emergency replacement equipment or to stock some intermediate inputs before an impending price rise, it might be impossible to get timely approval from the control authorities. In such cases a DFC, as the company's main financier and counsellor, could perform a valuable service, either as the advocate, or perhaps guarantor, of financing from the normal short-term lending source, or as the lender itself of the needed working capital. Obviously it would have to assess the need and be satisfied that the funds would be properly used. Its continuing familiarity with the company should make this easy, indeed foreseeable. With regard to normally successful exporting firms, the objective of maintaining their foreign exchange earnings would weigh heavily in the decision.

Input supply failures: Export producers generally depend considerably on the supply of local raw materials and other inputs, which are occasionally deficient in quantity, quality or both. Moreover, export producers are more vulnerable than domestically oriented manufactures to damage from such limitations, because their markets are more demanding about delivery schedules and quality. Hence, where such problems exist, they are a matter of concern to DFCs backing the export manufacturers, as well as (primarily) to the manufacturers themselves. The latter should, of course, bear the main responsibility for dealing with their non-performing suppliers, but they may occassionally need help from a financial ally.

Problems with foreign representative or customers: An export manufacturer might have trouble, or merely be dissatisfied, with his representation abroad, or he might lose a big customer. It would not be the DFC's job to replace the representative or to woo back the customer. But its contacts in the financial community abroad might be helpful to its client in diagnosing and overcoming the problem.

Declining export performance: The hypothetical exporter might be losing his market share through inadequate quality control, for example, or second rate style and finish. The DFC might become aware of this and be able to inform itself independently, through its access to an international financial network, of the problem as perceived in the foreign markets. It might thereby be better able to use its influence with the exporter (borrower) to secure an improvement in performance.

Commercial Banking

During the first development decades it was community thought that commercial banking in most developing countries was too imbued with foreign traditions and too wedded to short-term perspectives and collateral requirements to be an effective and reliable instrument for financing economic development. Hence, the creation and growth of specialized financial institutions, particularly DFCs. More recently, the pendulum has swung back somewhat, and commercial banks in a number of countries, under official pressure and a new generation of directors, have become more dynamic and development oriented (the State Bank of India is a notable example), and have been given special government resources for this purpose. Meanwhile DFCs (and other specialized banks) faced with unanticipated problems of foreign exchange fluctuations, mounting interest rates and arrears, have sometimes found it necessary to solicit deposits, engage in more lucrative money-market operations or merge with a commercial bank. The apparent trend is therefore now toward un versal banking.

Investment financing by commercial banks: The financing of investment by commercial banks is therefore no longer a rarity. However, since in the great majority of these banks, resources consist of deposits and other short-term fu ds, term lending remains a minor share of their total business. But that

Fertilizers	
Information requirements for importing chemical fertilizers	XIX/4 Oct-Dec 83 p. 22
Fish	
Market information on fish	XIX/3 July-Sept 83 p. 8
Flowers	
Tapping Europe's large floricultural market	XVI/4 Oct-Dec 80 p. 18
Fruit, Fruit Products	
The fruit juice trade an expanding business for developing countries	XVIII/4 Oct-Dec 82 p. 12
Key export openings for certain fresh fruits and vegetables	XVII/4 Oct-Dec 81 p. 14
Handling fresh tropical produce for export	XVII/1 Jan-Mar 81 p. 4
The Gulf States ripe for fruits and vegetables	XVII/1 Jan-Mar 81 p. 18
Hot line to the market	XVI/I Jan-Mar 80 p. 8
Handicrafts	
Philippine handicrafts: responding to the market	XVI/4 Oct-Dec 81 p. 6
Handicrafts marketing in the eighties	XVII/3 July-Sept 81 p. 4
Handicrafts: a case in promotion	XVII/3 July-Sept 81 p. 5
Herbal Drinks	
Herbal drinks—export prospects bright	XVII/1 Jan-Mar 81 p. 12
Leather Goods	
Entering the international leather goods market—advice for the new exporter	XIX/4 Oct-Dec 83 p. 8
Legumes	
Market openings in West Africa for cowpeas and Bambara groundnuts	XX/1 Jan-Mar 84 p. 14
Meats	
Horse and rabbit meat markets—possible outlets for exporters in developing countries	XIX/3 July-Sept 83 p. 11

Subject / Article	Reference
Medicinal Plants	
Botanicals–Increasing potential for pharmaceutical applications	XIX/2 Apr-June 83 p. 26
Pet Products	
Europe's dynamic market for pet products	XIX/3 July-Sept 83 p. 18
Seaweed	
Developing an export-oriented seaweed industry	XVIII/2 Apr.June 82 p. 12
Shrimps	
The shrimp trade-a big business for developing countries	XX/2 Apr-June 84 p. 4
Shrimps and prawns–a growing market in Western Europe	XVIII/2 Apr-June 82 p. 20
Spices	
The international spice trade: export opportunities for the rural sector	XIX/1 Jan-Mar 83 p. 4
Spices –a nontraditional export for micro-economies	XIX/1 Jan-Mar 83 p. 14
Spice promotion in the United States	XVI/3 July-Sept 80 p. 8
Textiles	
The importance of fashion in textile marketing	XVIII/3 July-Sept 82 p. 8
Tools	
Tool trade strong and expanding	XVII/3 July-Sept 81 p. 17
Vegetable Oils	
SIC's market intelligence system for oils and oilseeds	XVII/2 Apr-June 81 p. 4
Expanding mutual trade in vegetable oilseed products	XVII/2 Apr-June 81 p. 15
Vegetables, Vegetable Products	
Key export openings for certain fresh fruits and vegetables	XVII/4 Oct-Dec 81 p. 14
Dehydrated vegetables–careful marketing required	XVII/4 Oct-Dec 81 p. 22

Handling fresh tropical produce for export	XVII/1 Jan-Mar 81 p. 6
The Gulf states—ripe for fruits and vegetables	XVII/1 Jan-Mar 81 p. 18
Hot line to the market	XVI/1 Jan-Mar 80 p. 8
Wood Products	
Marketing prospects for wooden household furniture	XX/1 Jan-Mar 84 p. 4
Wooden building materials: attractive openings in Middle East market	XVIII/1 Jun-Mar 82 p. 8

---

total would exceed a DFC's operational volume many times over, party because most of the loan funds of commercial banks would turn over repeatedly, being repaid and relent, during the term of a single DFC transaction. When commercial banks do make term loans to finance investment, it may often be in cooperation with a DFC, the latter taking the longer debt maturities, while the banks are repaid on a shorter schedule.

Project appraisals by commercial banks are typically less elaborate than those undertaken by DFCS, as already indicated above, with more emphasis on collateral or formal guarantees and less on rate-of-return analyses. But in this respect also, their approaches are tending to converge. However when one or more banks join or cooperate with a DFC in financing a project, they are likely to base their review and decision on the DFC's appraisal.

Commercial banks' follow-up of projects would also usually involve less in-depth checking of performance and incipient problems than that of conscientious DFC management. This is partly, no doubt, because the commercial banks traditionally tend to rely more on receiving periodic reports from the client and ultimately on collateral security to safeguard their loan. But more particularly it is because the ba ks' involvement is less in overall terms, involving a more limited appraisal and shorter term commitment of funds (funds are usually attributed to specified items of equipment or to working capital needs, rather than to a total investment plan). Again, however, these differences seem to be less marked now than a decade ago. Likewise, commercial banks could probably be less prone than a DFC to make the lead in seeking and implementing solutions to the kinds of operational problems that have been cited above, although their help might well be enlisted by the DFC as part of the solution.

Export credit: In the limited sense of financing only the actual export transaction, export credit is a major part of the operational volume of many commercial banks and constitutes almost the entire business of specialized export banks where they have been established. It involves essentially automatic advances against specified documents confirming an export order, and subsequent progressive liquidation of these advances as payments are made (from a letter of credit or otherwise) in accordance with the sales contract, against other documents certifying shipment, delivery, inspection and so on of the goods. This voluminous documentation is generated by a host of banks around the world, which are linked by formal correspondent, commission-sharing relationships, and is standardized to a high degree. Thus it is relatively easy for a bank clerk in Thailand or Trinidad, for example, to check a letter of credit or bill of lading originating in India. But he must do so attentively, for payments contravening the contract could be costly. Because the business is routine and its volume is very large, the margins are small although profitable, and the risks are minimal, well secured and usually guaranteed by the government.

Nonfinancial services: Adequate and timely financing is the form of assistance most often called for by exporters and governments from financial institutions. Yet financial incentives and facilities will seldom prove to be effective in the absence of a technically sound export product (defined as one suited to its intended market) supported by a substantial measure of commercial motivation and marketing skill. Many developing countries are seeking to build up these technical and commercial capabilities in a variety of ways—for instance by creating design centres, or by providing training in quality control, entrepreneurship, business management, market research and sales promotion—in parallel with financing programmes or under the aegis of the financial institutions.

There tend to be certain advantages of using financial institutions to provide such export services as opposed to using independent consultants. One is that an export producer needing help in the design, adaptation or marketing of his product, or in the management of his finances, may be more likely to follow the advice given by a technical assistance unit closely linked with his financing source than he would similar guidance offered by a no less qualified unaffiliated consultant. Of more importance is the fact that the financially linked unit has the backing of an organization with considerable expertise and business contacts. Through that organization, moreover, the unit usually has a preferred access to an extensive financial and information network that might be of considerable value in resolving the client's problems or in promoting his commercial interests.

On the other hand, such a financially linked export advisory unit might neglect the exploration of other possible networks that an independent export consultant would consider of equal or even more importance to solving the export problem. Moreover, it is sometimes suggested that an advisory unit's explicit organizational link with a financial institution may give rise to other problems, such as bureaucratic rivalries between the technical and financial branches; undue expectations of the client on the ready access to finance; and the suspicion of bias in project appraisals, favouring those helped by the advisory unit. On balance, however, such doubts would seem to be outweighed by the likely advantages, including needed financial support, of using the advisory unit linked to a financial institution.

In any event, industrial and export-financing institutions (principally DFCs) in a number of countries have established export advisory units to help their clients—sometimes non-clients as well-with business management problems of various kinds. These units are not usually intended to promote only export production and sales, but rather to foster industrial development more generally, because their expertise is relevant for both domestic and export requirements. This expertise is more and more in demand for export projects, as such projects receive increasingly higher priority in many countries and are recognized as posing more complex problems than domestic business ventures.

4

THE BANKING SYSTEM: ITS ROLE IN EXPORT DEVELOPMENT

D.P. GUPTA*

Institutions in a country's banking system—the central bank, commercial banks and development banks—all have a trade promotion role. Banks in many developing countries play a relatively limited role in the national trade promotion effort. They often consider that it is the business of the government and of exporters to work out strategies for developing and promoting exports. In cases where the banking system does provide a certain degree of support to the export drive, these financial institutions frequently operate within narrow limits and may work according to conservative or traditional procedures. As a result, exporters in those countries do not have the banking services that are taken for granted by exporters in most developed countries.

There are, however, some exceptions. In certain developing countries countries the financial institutions have become active partners in the export process, working jointly with other trade promotion institutions. Exporters in these countries can

*D.P. Gupta is ITC's export financing adviser.

approach their banks for assistance and be assured of receiving the required help. This type of support has been one of the most important factors behind the successful export performance of such countries and territories as Argentina, Brazil, Hong Kong, India, the Republic of Korea, Singapore and Yugoslavia, among others.

In the highly competitive international marketing situation that exists today, exporters must receive adequate support from their financial institutions if they are to perform successfully. It is thus imperative that their banks study the services needed by the export community and see how they can provide and improve them.

The Banking System in Developing Countries

The three types of financial institutions the generally exist in the banking system of a developing country and are concerned with the trade and manufacturing sectors are central banks, commercial-banks and development banks. The functions of these are generally considered to be the following:

1. Central banks manage the currency, the public debt and the foreign exchange reserves of the country.

2. Commercial banks collect deposits and make short-term loans to individuals and institutions in the country.

3. Development banks make medium and long-term loans to the industrial sector from funds received primariiy through governments budgesary allocations and international financial institutions.

In addition to these standard, or more tradtional responsibilities, however, these organisations could make a concerted ellort to introduce financial and non-financial services to develop and promote the country's exports. Each of these institutions—the central bank, the commerical bank and the development banks—has a distinctive role to play in this context, with the central bank seeing as the coordinating agency among them.

Role of Central Banks

Central banks have a domminant role to play in export financing. Yet in many developing countries their export financing functions have been passive. Many of them have no special schemes for developing and promoting exports. Some central banks do not take an active part in assisting the export sector on the grounds that such a role is not strictly a legitimate central banking function. In a developing economy, however, a central bank should formulate its policies and gear its operations so as to find solutions to the country's overall economic problems. Highly specicalized trade promotion activities should therefore be regarded as among these legitimate banking functions—even if they appear unorthodox from the central bank's point of view. In certain developed and developing countries central banks have followed such positive policies to the advantage of the export community, as well as to the country as a whole.

In the interest of trade promotion, a central bank should consider undertaking the following types of activities:

1. Study the commercial banks' export credit policies on a product-by-product basis, since export financing problems vary from one item to another.

2. Discuss the results, of these studies with commeircial banks and assist them to formulate special schemes for granting adequate financing to exporters at the pre and post-shipment stages, at concessional rates of interest.

3. Introduce a special scheme loans granted by commercial and development banks to the export sector, for example by ensuring a reasonable margin between the commercial and development banks' lending rates and the cost of the central bank's refinancing facility.

4. Allow the commercial banks to go above their normal credit ceiling (if one exists) in order to grant export loans.

5. Collect statistics periodically from the commercial banks on the export financing that they grant, to use as a basis for making policy decisions on export loans.

6. Establish a special export credit unit within the central bank to study the financial and nonfinancial problems of the export sector and to suggest and implement remedial measures.

7. Study the advisability and feasibility of setting up a special department within the central bank of elsewhere, for introducing export credit guarantee and insurance schemes.

Role of Commercial Bank

Commercial banks are one of the main pillars in national trade promotion efforts Unfortunately, in many developing countries their role vis-a-vis the commercial sector has evolved as primarily one of financing their customers' domestic business. Furthermore, they have often not become involved to non-financial services, which can be especially useful for exporters.

New and small exporters in developing countries in particular often face major problems in getting financing from their banks. They have difficulty passing the rigid tests to qualify for loans, even if they are fully capable of complying with the terms of their export contracts. They are also of a disadvantage when seeking financing because they often lack tangible security, their export transactions may yield comparatively small returns and they face the general risks inherent in exporting. Exporters must receive adequate support from financial bodies if they are to perform successfully.

Commercial banks in many developing countries need to make a conscious effort to assist the export sector. A bank's services for exporters can be divided into two categories, financial and nonfinancial services. Banks and trade promotion agencies have a complementary role in trade promotion.

Financial Services

In recent years many developing countries have started to diversify their export range to include new types of products. In the past, they exported mainly commodities and raw materials, which they sold in traditional buyers in traditional markets. Such exports, required no special type of financing arrangements. But as developing countries increasingly, try to penetrate new markets and diversify their export product mix, they need more complex and comprehensive financial support from the banks. Furthermore, for products exported in bulk. Importers often demand various facilities such as storage and soft-credit terms, which also require additional financing services. Some developing countries have begun to export heavy equipment and turnkey projects, and to execute construction works, which likewise call for suitable financing arrangements. If the banks cannot support such exporters through satisfactory services, the exports cannot even bid on such contracts.

New and small exporters often face major difficulties on getting financting from their banks. Banks in developing countries therefore need to make changes in their operational policies and procedural formalities to help their clients attract export business and make their goods available at competitive prices abroad. Equally important are the terms and conditions of the credit. Financial assistance should be provided to exporters in the amount needed, within the necessary time period and on the terms required. Facilities should be made available to exporters in the small-scale business sector as well as to large firms, and to export merchants as well as export-manufacturers. Because financial problems vary with the type of export products, banks should work out operational mechanisms to meet the requirements of exporters handing different types of items.

Stages of financing: Exporters require financial services at four different stages of their export operations: at the pre-tender and stages, in the case of contract bidding, and at the pre-shipment and post-shipment stages, for the production of export goods. During each of these phases exporters need different types of financial assistance, depending on the nature of the export contract. Bank services are required in the first two stages for comparatively large exports.

Pre-shipment financing: Pre-shipment credits are usually more important to exporters in developing countries than other types of credit. Banks should therefore consider introducing special schemes for advancing funds of the pre-shipment stage.

Some developing countries already operate such arrangements that are working quite satisfactorily. Others, however, have schemes that are not used extensively because of their rigid formalities and time-consuming procedures. For example, if it takes the bank a long time to approve credit, the manufacturer's production programme can be upset and he may be prevented from following the stipulated shipping schedule for the export order. Exporters frequently suffer heavy losses, sometimes even cancellation of contracts, because of a delay in receiving preshipment funds from their banks. Furthermore, in many developing countries no pre-shipment financing schemes exist at all.

Some export financing schemes are not used because of their rigid formalities. It is important for a developing country to introduce a simple and flexible scheme so that exporters can use it easily. The salient features of a simple arrangement of this type are the following:

Eligibility: Exporters of all products other than those such as mineral fuels, sugar and other commodities that are exported as cash items.

Coverage: 80 per cent 9C to per cent of the value of the export contract. If the exporter has received an advance or a down payment from the importer, this should be taken into consideration, as should the expected profits of the export transaction.

Rate of interest: A preferential rate, which could be 2 per cent below the discount rate of the central bank.

Period of credit: Not exceeding one year.

Nature of the advances: Overdrafts, packing credits or pre-shipment loans. depending on the goods being financed and the nature of the export sales contract.

Type of security or collateral: Firm orders or contracts of sale under letters of credit, on approved credit terms or according to generally acceptable international practices. Also, export credit guarantee and insurance policies.

Repayment: Negotiation, purchase or discount of the export bills.

Post-shipment credit: Pre-shipment credits are generally extinguished by either negotiating export bills or sanctioning post-shipment credits against the purchase or discount of export bills. Such credits should be made available liberally, covering up to 80 per cent or 90 per cent of the export bill. They should be granted at the same concessional rates of interest as pre-shipment finance. The credit period should extent from the time of shipment until receipt of the export proceeds. Since most export from developing countries are on a short-term basis, the loan period will not generally exceed six months.

Guarantees: Guarantees may be required at the various stages of export financing for different purposes, such as:

1. For a contractor at the time of submitting a quotation for tender in a foreign country.

2. For a foreign contractor when a contract has been awarded, to cover the exporter's due performance of the contract.

3. For the importer abroad as coverage for an advance payment he has made to the exporter.

4. For an importer in lieu of retention money for satisfactory performance of the items supplied for a stipulated period.

5. For customs, tax and other authorities for the purposes of clearance of raw material from a bonded warehoure, payment of various taxes such as sales tax and excise duties, and so on.

Such guarantees are generally issued by commercial banks. Unless guarantee facilities are made available to export liberally without rigid formalities, export promotion efforts are bound to suffer.

Easing the requirements for letters of credit: Exports from developing countries are generally made against letters of credit (L/Cs). However it is becoming more difficult for exporters to get L/Cs established, particularly from importers in developed countries. because of the added costs involved in opening a letter of credit as compared with other terms of payment. Banks will not generally give financial assistance to exporters unless their export transactions are fully covered by L/Cs and also usually only if the letters of credit are confirmed. Banks tend to look unfavourably upon export transactions carried out on the basis of documents against payment (D/P), document against acceptance (D/A) or consignment selling. The bank's export financing facility is therefore extended in a very restricted manner and is used mainly by large, established exporters with confirmed letters of credit.

Banks should make it a policy to grant credit to exporters at the pre-shipment stage even without letters of credit. This will allow the exporters to procure raw materials. cover their processing costs and pay for the packing, freight and insurance for their export operations. In following such a procedure the banks can base their loan decisions on the existence of firm orders or contracts of sale, as well as on the exporter's capability and integrity, rather than on the existence of an L/C.

Equal treatment for export merchants: In most developing countries there are a considerable number of small export merchants in addition to export manufacturers. Although the share of export merchants in the country's foreign trade may not be substantial in terms of volume and value, it would be wrong to underestimate their importance in the national export effort. Export merchants usually buy, rather than produce, goods for export. They need pre-shipment financing to procure the goods, arrange for packaging, give advances against the manufacture of the goods, and cover freight and insurance. They should therefore be provided with the same type of banking facilities that are available to export-manufacturers. In quite a few developing countries, however, advances to export merchants are treated as normal bank loans, and they are charged higher rates of interest, as well as a higher security margin, than loans to export manufacturers. In the interest of trade promotion, commercial banks should do away with such a distinction.

Simplifying procedures: To make the export financing process run more smoothly, a commercial bank's management should give officers at various levels in the headquarters and in branches adequate discretionary powers to grant export credits as well as guarantee facilities on their own authority. Appropriate mechanisms should be established to verify that the officers are actually using such powers effectively. The head office should also issue detailed guidelines for its officers on important operational matters related to export financing such as the margins to be applied in L/C and non-L/C cases; the method of checking various export documents submitted for the negotiation purchase or discount of export bills; the procedure for providing forward exchange cover; and so on.

Nonfinancial Services

A bank's nonfinancial services are as important to exporters as financial servicas. Such services include counselling exporters on shipping documents, foreign exchange regulations, forward exchange cover, contract documents, customs laws and the credit rating of buyers and agents.

For example, exporters sometimes ship goods without being aware of the exchange control regulations in the buyer's country. They may therefore face undue delay in receiving their export proceeds. Or they may need expert advice before submitting documents for international competitive bidding.

Some of the nonfinancial services could also be provided by national trade promotion agencies through an up to date information base serviced through embassies and other channels. Banks could likewise disseminate important information of a general nature through trade promotion agencies. In other words, in trade promotion and export development efforts, banks and trade promotion agencies have a complementary role and they should therefore develop close working relationships.

Banks could bring out information booklets, preferably with national trade promotion organizations, on a wide selection of topies, such as common discrepancies in export documents, terms used in export business and measures to take against exchange risks. This could benefit the export community considerably and in the long run could help the banks a swell. For example, guidance on exchange risks and common discrepancies in documents could enable exporters to take precautions at the initial stages of their export operations, thereby assisting the commercial banks to process export documents more expeditiously.

Developed countries and some developing countries have introduced such services to assure a rapid and complete receipt of export proceeds, as well as to educate the export community. These services have been found to be extremely helpful to exporters in diversifying export products and markets.

Role of Development Banks

The government should set up arrangements to encourage banks to lend to exporters. Development banks have been created in many countries mainly to term loans for setting up, diversifying and expanding industrial projects. They are also often expected to render merchant bank types of services for developing the industrial infrastructure. In practice, however, most of these banks are engaged mainy in financing development projects, often in a complex manner, and they have no special schemes for promoting, developing and servicing export-oriented industries. If export performance is to be improved, development banks must introduce such special schemes, as well as related services to assist the export sector.

The following are some of the export-related projects that development banks could consider financing:

1. Industrial estates could be set up exclusively for export-oriented firms with facilities such as electricity, water and telephone services provided.

2. Projects for export-oriented industries could be considered on a priority basis, and certain of the standard financial conditions for loans could be eased for them. For example, the debt-equity ratio for the loan could be relaxed for such projects and only a certain percentage of the standard interest could be charged during the construction stage of the new industry with the balance to be paid when the project went into commercial production.

3. Because of uncertainties in getting supplies of inputs for their export products, due to problems in transport arrangements, exporters in many developing countries are obliged to maintain inventories of their component materials for up to six months. This gives them the assurance that they can keep their assembly line going uninterrupted to meet their export schedule. Commercial banks generally finance only up to two or three months' of stock, resulting in a heavy burden on exporters.

Development banks could participate with commercial banks in financing such inventories for the extended period.

4. Many development banks have lines of credit in foreign currencies with international and regional institutions. To assist exporters to buy stocks of inputs for export products on a forward contract basis, development banks could make special arrangements with these institutions to use the credit line for this purpose.

5. A scheme could be set up to provide seed capital to technically qualified and experienced persons and companies that do not have adequate financial resources for establishing export-oriented industries. National trade promotion organizations have a major role to play in identifying companies and markets with export potential and in providing approriate support services.

6. The development bank could arrange technical or financial cooperation arrangements with reputable foreign manufacturers, including through the UN Industrial Development Organization (UNIDO), development banks abroad and other institutions that help organize foreign joint ventures.

Supporting Measures by Governments

The promotion and development of exports is a joint endeavour of the government, banks and other trade servicing institutions, on the one hand, and exporters, on the other. The functions of banks vis-à-vis exporters have been broadly discussed above. For banks to provide satisfactory services to exports, governments must initiate certain policies and support schemes. The following are some of the measures that developing countries with successful export performance have found helpful in this respect.

1. Interest rate policy: When formulating-policies on the interest rates that banks are to change for various types of export loans, government authorities should consider the effect

of such rates on the export cost as well as on the competitiveness of the country's exporters compared with their counterparts in other countries. It may be necessary for the government to subsidize the interest rates so that banks can charge lower rates to exporters. This could be done other through a refinancing mechanism of the central bank (for example, a margin of 2½ per cent to 3 per cent could be allowed between the commercial banks' lending rates and the central banks' refinancing rates), or by directly subsidizing the commercial banks to facilitate lending to the export sector at lower rates.

2. Export credit guarantee and insurance schemes: Many developed countries, as well as a small number of developing countries, consider such schemes to be one of their most important trade promotion tools. The primary role of commercial banks is to serve as the custodian for their depositors' funds. If, in addition, as a promotional measure, banks lend funds to exporters more liberally and on softer terms, a specialized export credit guarantee and insurance agency, such as those already operating in many countries, should be able to take a major portion of the risks that banks incur in such lending. The government should, therefore, institute appropriate arrangements to encourage commercial banks to lend to the export sector. Such schemes could be introduced by the central bank or the development bank as the agent of the government.

3. Financing of incentives: Many developing countries provide incentives to exporters such as duty drawback, cash assistance and tax rebate. The procedural mechanism for taking advantage of such incentives needs to be simplified in most countries to make these arrangements effective. In some countries, governments have authorized commercial banks to reimburse exporters under such schemes when they negotiate, discount or purchase the export documents. The commercial banks can later claim reimbursement from the central bank.

4. Loans or grants to development banks: To assist development banks to build industrial estates and finance inventories,

governments can make funds available to them as grants or loans on very soft terms.

5. Repatriation of export proceeds: Exchange control regulations in many developing countries require that export proceeds be repatriated within six months. Exceptions are often allowed for capital goods exports. However, exchange control regulations may have to be relaxed for certain types of exports, because export proceeds do not always arrive within the six-month period.

6. Exchange rate policy: The exchange rate policy has a great impact on the trade promotion efforts of a country. It is in this domain that the central banks should assist the governments in formulating a realistic policy to be implemented through the banking system.

Conclusion

Export financing is a highly complex area that requires skill and expertise in financial operations as well as a thorough knowledge of the export process and of the conditions prevailing in the international market. This article has touched upon some of the general problems that developing countries face in insitituting a useful and efficient export financing system. In establishing its own national export financing framework, each government should study the issues raised, in relation to the country's particular foreign trade situation, to arrive at services that will effectively support the export community.

5

PROTECTING YOUR PRODUCT

DON WELLER*

If your company has developed a new product or established its trade name, you may decide to seek legal protection to prevent others from copying it. At some point during the development of a new product, a company will often face the question: "Can and should we protect it from being copied?" The problem arises not only when a company has developed a product with original features, but also when it has established its trade name to the point where it has earned buyer recognition and respect, and therefore has marketable value.

Legal protection for products is a highly complicated field, and when the question arises a company should use a specialized lawyer. But company managers should have a good general idea of the kinds of legal protection available.

*Pon Weller is principal lecturer international marketing at North Staffordshire Polytechnic in the United Kingdom and a writer on marketing. He was assisted in preparing this series by Michael Clements, senior lecturer in marketing at the same institution. This article is based on excerpts from ITC's textbook Export Product Development, which is a component of Pack 8 in ITC's series of training packs, @ ITC..

Forms of Protection

The relevant laws vary significantly from country to country, but basically there are four legal forms of protection; patents, trademarks, registration of industrial designs and copyrights.

Patents: If a product (or also usually a process) can be legally qualified as an "invention," then a patent is the best form of protection.

Under most national patent legislation, a product (or process) must fulfill three basic conditions to be patentable:

It must be new in the sense that there is no indication that is has already been published or publicly used.

It must be nonobvious in the sense that it involves an inventive step and would not have occurred to a specialist in the particular industrial field, had he been asked to find a solution to a particular problem.

It must be applicable in industry, in the sense that it can be industrially manufactured or used.

A patent is a document, issued by a governmental authority, which describes an invention. It creates a legal situation in which the invention can normally be exploited (made, imported, sold, used) only by the patent owner or with his authorization.

A patent provides the manufacturer with a monopoly for his product (or process, and, in that case, frequently also the product directly obtained from the process) for a relatively long period (usually 15 to 20 years) and makes it difficult for a would be competitor to copy or imitate the product (or process) without making substantial improvements. On the other hand, obtaining a patent in each target market can be an expensive undertaking, particularly if there are several markets and not all of them can be covered through one of the existing multi-country patent agreements discussed later in this article.

Registration of industrial designs: From the legal viewpoint, the industrial design of a product relates to its visual design (its shape, colour and so on) rather than to how it functions.

If the design of a product is novel primarily because of its appearance rather than any functional features, registering the design may be the most suitable form of protection, in countries where it is possible. (In the United States this is known as a design patent.) A registered design may not be copied or imitated without the registered owner's authorizations, and unauthorized copies or imitations may not be sold or imported. Protection usually ranges between five and fifteen years, but it is generally renewable.

But the protection actually offered by registering an industrial design is often questionable at best. Very slight modifications are often enough to create a "new" design in the eyes of the law. If a company brings out a successful product with a novel appearance, it can be reasonably sure that cheaper copies will appear on the market sooner or later; they may be different enough from the original to evade legal action, but the differences may be so subtle that many customers may overlook them, or accept them because of the lower price.

This does not mean it is useless to bring out products with original designs. Companies that do so tend to be the most successful. But they achieve their success by such means as introducing new designs often enough to keep a step ahead of the copiers, offering products which are superior in quality or function, establishing a strong brand identity which people value and trust, offering better service than copiers, building up a superior distribution network and so on.

Trademark registration: A trademark is a sign or symbol that serves to distinguish a company's products or services. It may consist of one or more distinctive words, letters, numbers, drawings or pictures, emblems, signatures, or even colours or combinations of colours. Under the trademark legislation of many countries, a trademark may also consist of the form or other special features of a product's container or package, provided that they are not solely dictated by their function.

Trademark registration is of practical value especially if the producer or marketer can develop a unique trademark and establish its value with buyers. A good example is the "Coke" name and bottle, with its special shape. Both are registered in all countries where the soft drink is sold.

Registering a trademark (usually with the same government authority that issues patents) is much cheaper than obtaining a patent or registering a design. In some cases, a trademark may be protected without registration.

Once a trademark has been protected, no person or enterprise other than its owner may use it or any trademark that is so similar to it that its use would lead to confusion in the minds of the public.

The protection of a trademark is usually not limited in time, but in most countries its registration has to be renewed perfectually.

Copyright: Copyright offers protection for what are legally described as "literary and artistic works." Most nationally copyright laws provide for the protection of literary, musical, artistic and photographic works; maps and technical drawings; and motion pictures. Many copyright laws also protect "works of applied art," such as artistic jewellery, lamps, wallpaper and furniture.

Manufacturers also commonly rely on copyright protection for package designs, toys and games. Copyright is also used to protect the design drawings of models of new products, although it does not protect the product itself.

In fact, copyright is a very limited form of protection even for products such as those mentioned above. In many countries it is not recognized as a legal form of protection for many types of product, such as furniture and jewellery. Moreover, infringement of a copyright may be hard to prove, since in most countries copyright is automatic and does not involve registration.

Industrial Protection

All of the above forms of protection are basically national; they confer rights granted by an individual country and are valid only within that country. So before marketing a new product internationally, a company must decide which markets are or may become significant to it, and then secure a patent and/or other form of protection in each of them.

Most industrialized countries and many others are signatories to various international agreements within the framework of the Paris Convention for the Protection of Industrial Property. which has been important in helping companies to secure protection for their products in foreign markets.

Among the more important provisions of the paris Convention:

Foreign companies* have equal rights to potent, trademark and other protection as domestic firms.

If an invention, design or other form of industrial property qualifies for protection, foreign owners* are entitled to such protection even though they may not have applied for it in their own countries.

If a person or company* files an application for protection in one signatory country, it has priority for a certain period of time (six or twelve months) in all signatory countries over applications filed during that period by the other persons for

*The benefits of the Parts Convention apply to natural and legal persons who are nationals of a contracting state or who are domielled or have a real and effective industrial or commercial establishment in such a state.

protection of the same invention, design, trademark and so on.

Each signatory state must maintain a special industrial property service, which must inform the public of patents, utility models, trademarks and industrial designs and publish an official journal. The journal must contain the names of the owners of the patents granted, with a brief description of the patented inventions and the reproduction of every registered trademark.

Both the national office and its journal are essential sources of information for companies seeking data about the current state of the art for a particular product which they may intend to develop.

But the problem remains that each country's legislation on protection of industrial property varies, so a form of protection that is perfectly satisfactory for a product in one country may not be effective in others in which a company intends to sell. Moreover, even though a company secures protection in one country, it may not get it in another.

Searches

The first step in securing protection is usually to conduct a search to see whether the invention, design or trademark is not already legally protected in the markets in which a company is interested. The major exception is copyright, which is usually granted automatically without formal procedures. Once the search establishes that the invention, design or trademark does not infringe on anyone else's, the next step is to file appropriate applications. Many of today's manufactures are designs once patented and now copied by thousands of manufacturers.

Search benefits: Particularly in the case of a patent search, the procedure can turn up valuable information for a company. For example, besides revealing whether certain features of a product have already been protected such a search will give a detailed picture of the current state of the art for the particular type of product. This information can be invaluable for the further refinement and improvement of a company's present product.

Should a search reveal that the manufacturer's product does infringe on existing patents or registered designs, the company may be able to modify the product and avoid such infringement. If such changes lead to improvements over the original protected product, its manufacturer might well request a license to incorporate the improvements inh is own product. In many cases, two manufacturers cross-license each other as a means of protecting their inventions and designs from possible infringement by others. Cross-licensing involves the exchange of manufacturing rights for the protected features of the product that each manufacturer has developed independently.

Another benefit in conducting a search is that a manufacturer will often learn of product features that may no longer be legally protected and which he can incorporate in his own product. As noted above, patents usually expire after 15 to 20 years, and registrations of a design after about five years in many countries. Once they expire, the invention or design can be copied without danger of infringement. A majority of the world's manufactures today consist of inventions and designs that were once patented or registered but whose protection has long since expired and are copied by literally thousands of manufacturers, who thus save the expense of developing their own inventions and designs.

National searches: In some industrialized countries the national patent office will conduct a search for a fee, which will tell the manufacture.

Whether his product is patentable in the country in question.

The prior state of the art in his product category.

Who has already obtained a patent or registered a design for the same or a similar product.

Not all national patent offices offer a search service to the public. In the United States, for example, such a service is not offered. Instead, patent attorneys (called "patent agents" in most other English-speaking countries) use the facilities of the U.S. Patent Office to conduct such searches on behalf of their clients.

The cost of a search varies greatly, depending upon the type of search that is needed. This, in turn, is usually dictated by the nature of the product. For example, if an invention can be easily categorized, then the cost of each national search might be only $500 or $600. In more complicated cases the cost can be much higher. Once translations and other charges are added in, the cost of obtaining a patent can run to several thousand dollars in each country.

International Protection

Fortunately, as a result of relatively recent international agreements, the cost and complexity of obtaining multi-country patent protection has been reduced in many cases. Two of these agreements are already in operation and a third is on the way.

The Patent Cooperation Treaty: The Patent Cooperation Treaty (PCT) went into effect in 1978. At the end of 1981, a total of 32 countries had adhered to it. The PCT provides for the filing of a single "international application" when protection is sought for an invention in several countries simultaneously. This has the same effect as if applications had been filed separately in each of the countries in which protection is sought. An international application can usually be filed with the national officer of the applicant (or the European Patent Office; see below) and is filed in one single language. Because the international application is prepared in accordance with international standards effective in all of the PCT contracting states, subsequent amendments because of varying national requirements and the costs associated therewith) will not become necessary. Moreover, a single cost is incurred for preparing and filing an international application.

Each international application is subjected to a search to discover "prior art." The search is conducted by one of the International Searching Authorities, namely the Patent Offices of Australia, Austria, Japan, Sweden or the United States; the USSR State Committee; or the European Patent Office.

If specially requested by the applicant, and provided the interested contracting state permits, the international application is also subjected to a preliminary examination to find out out whether the invention seems to be new, nonobvious and industrially applicable. The preliminary examination is carried out by one of the international Examining Authorities, namely the Patent Offices of Australia, Austria, Japan, Sweden, the United Kingdom, the USSR State Committee and the European Patent Office.

The international application, together with the international search report, is generally published upon the expiration of 18 months from the date of filing of the international application for, where priority of an earlier application is claimed, from the filling date of that application). This international publication is accepted by most PCT contracting states as equivalent to a national publication (subject, in some cases, to compliance with further conditions) for the purposes of affording provisional protection to the claimed invention.

The advantages offered by the PCT are many. One international application in one single language can replace multiple national applications in several languages in the majority of industrialized countries as well as in many developing countries. A European patent application can also be filed via the PCT, which combines the advantages of both the PCT and the European Patent Convention.

Once the relevant reports have been established—and not before—the application is processed separately in the various countries, each of which will then grant or refuse protection. These reports give the applicant a solid basis to evaluate his chances of obtaining patents in the various countries and, if his chances are not favourable, to decide not to proceed further with his applications, thus avoiding costs in preparing translations, appointing agents, paying national fees and so on.

The PCT also offers a major advantage for inventors and companies that are not certain about the commercial success of their inventions. When a patent application is filed through the PCT, the national procedure for the grant of a patent is delayed for 20 months in all cases and 25 months if preliminary examination is requested. Should the search report and/or the preliminary examination report turn out to be unfavourable, the company saves the time and money that it would have otherwise spent on the filing and processing of patent applications with different national offices.

The European Patent Convention: The European Patent Convention (EPC) started operating in 1978. Since then 11 of the 16 signatory states have adhered to the Convention. The EPC established the European Patent Office, localed in Munich. Federal Republic of Germany, which grants a European Patent on the basis of a single application. This patent has the effect of a national patent in all contracting states in which the applicant desires to have patent protection. This patent can also be obtained by nationals and residents of nonmember states.

The advantages of the EPC for the owner of an invention are obvious. For example, to obtain protection in the United Kingdom, France, Sweden and Switzerland, a separate application must be filed in each country. This means coping with four different languages, laws and procedures. If patents are required in other European countries as well, which is often the case, the problems are magnified.

Under the EPC, however only one application is needed, and this can be processed in a single language (English, French or German), following only one law and procedure.

An application for a European Patent may be filed at the European Patent Office or at the national patent offices in the contracting states. It is then subjected to a formalities examination, mainly to ensure that the documents submitted satisfy the requirements of publication. A parallel search is carried out to discover prior publications which may affect the novelty or obviousness of the invention defined in the application. Shortly afterwards the application, together with the search report, is published. This eliminates a long delay before the contents of patent specifications are disclosed to the public.

Once he has received the search report, the applicant can decide in the light of its findings whether he wishes to pursue his application further, if he does nothing the application is considered as withdrawn. Although the applicant obtains only provisional protection his published application will effectively establish prior art against later applications in respect of the same subject matter.

Should the applicant wish to proceed, he must file a request for examination. This may be done at any time up to six months after the search report has been published. The application is examined by the European Patent Office to determine whether it satisfies the requirements for patentability laid down in the EPC.

Before any decision is taken by the Office, the applicant will have the opportunity to submit amendments and to discuss with the examiner concerned any difficulties that may arise. Should the examiner refuse to grant a patent, the applicant may turn to a Board of Appeal, the independence of whose members is safeguarded by the terms of the convention.

The introduction of the Eurpean Patent has led to a significant decrease in the cost of patenting an invention in Europe. The costs shown above for obtaining a European. Patent, when added together, are less than the total of comparable fees for obtaining a single national patent in any one of several European countries.

A European Patent has the same effect and is subject to the same condition as a national patent in all contracting states in which the applicant has requested patent protection, with these important exceptions:

The Europen Patent for each country will have a uniform term of 20 years from the date of filing of the European application.

By filing a notice within nine months following the grant of a patent, it is possible for a competitor to oppose, by a single action taken in the European Patent Office, a patent granted for all of the signatory countries.

The patent may at any time during its life be revoked in any country, but only on grounds specified in the convention.

Community Patent Convention: This convention was signed by the nine member states of the European Community (EC) in 1975 but has not yet come into effect. It will create a single patent valid for all EC countries and a uniform patent law.

Under the convention, products protected by the Community patent will circulate freely once the owner of the patent or someone with his consent has marketed them in any part of the EC.

Applications for patents under the EC Convention will be processed by the European Patent Office in Munich.

Information Sources

Even with these international agreements securing patents or other forms of protection for new products in foreign markets is a complex undertaking. Companies should use patent attorneys who are familiar with the relevant national legislation and with the international agreements. If a company uses an attorney in its own country, it should be sure that he has connections in the target markets, and is experienced in the field of industrial property.

Usually it is best to use an attorney who is located in the market region. For example, an Asian manufacturer that wants patent protection in several European markets might use a legal firm which is headquartered in one European centre and has agents throughout the area. In many industrized countries, patent attorneys have to undergo specialized training and pass qualifying examinations. The industrial property offices of those countries keep up-to-date lists of such qualified patent attorneys and will send a copy upon request.

But before a company commissions a patent attorney, it can inform itself of possible infringement problems that it might face. The sources of information described below are not a substitute for the professional services of a qualified attorney, but they can help to decide, for example, whether to seek protection in certain markets. These sources may also provide information about products already on the market, which may be useful for the company's research and developmenl staff.

National sources: Every signatory state of the Paris Convention issues a journal that gives complete information about patents granted and trademark and industrial designs registered in the county. This official journal is published by each country's national industrial property office, which will send upon request details concerning the full range of information services available as well as the procedures to be followed when applying for the various forms of protection available, the costs involved and necessary forms.

A company can obtain the addresses of these offices from local diplomatic missions or from its own country's industrial property office. Many such offices maintain a file of information about industrial property regulations and procedures of the major industrial countries.

World Intellectual Property Organization: The World Intellectual Property Organization (WIPO) is a specialized agency of the UN. Many of its activities are devoted to assisting developing countries, particularly in the transfer of technology and known how.

WIPO's international Bureau operates several service that are of possible use to many companies developing new products and trademarks, including trademark and industrial design registration services.

The International Registration of Trademarks Service has recorded nearly half a million registrations and renewals since it was set up in 1893. It publishes an official monthly bulletin. Les Marques Internationales, which contains information about newly registered trademarks, renewals and changes in earlier registrations.

On request, the service delivers certified copies of registrations, and for a fee it conducts international trademark searches.

WIPO's International Deposit of Industrial Designs Service has registered nearly 70,000 designs since it was established in 1982. The Service issues the monthly Bulletin des Dessin set Modeles Internationaux, in which are published all new registrations and any changes in earlier registrations.

WIPO also operates free-of-charge patent documentation and information services to institutions and individuals in developing countries, which provide worldwide technical information in all fields of technology where industrially applicable inventions are made. The services are offered by contributing industrial property offices under agreements concluded between those offices and WIPO, and include state-of-the art searches, procurement of individual copies of patent documents as well as legal status information on existing patents.

The International Bureau of WIPO has a central administrative role in the application of the Patent Cooperation Treaty. It keeps copies of and publishes all the international applications filed under the treaty, and also publishes the PCT Gazette.

WIPO's monthly review, Industrial Property, is a useful source of information. It can be ordered dierctly from WIPO. Further details of the above and other activities of WIPO can be obtained by writing to WIPO, 32 Chemin des Colombettes. CH-1211 Geneva 20, Switzerland.

International Patent Documentation Centre: Since 1972, the International Patent Documentation Centre (INPADOC) has operated a computerized bibliographic data exchange system under an agreement between Austria and WIPO. This is a worldwide data bank that contains basic bibliographie data on eight million patent documents. About 800,000 newly published patent documents are added each year. It regularly receives inputs from 50 participating offices, which together account for 95 per cent of the world total of published patent documents.

INPADOC provides regular services based on this system, including bibliographies, indices, standard profiles, magnetic type services, microfiches, and question-and-answer services.

Information about these services can be obtained from the International Patent Documentation Centre. Mollwaldplatz 4, A—1040, Vienna, Austria.

Other Information Sources

Apart from the above, official, sources of information concerning patents and other forms of industrial property, may commercial sources provide technical services based either wholly or in part upon patent documents. These take the form of specially commissioned searches, alerting services or biblographic referral service. There is a growing tendency to offer one line computer files searchable over international data switching networks that complement the traditional publication on paper.

6

EXPORT MARKETING TECHNIQUES

I

EXPORTING CONSUMER GOODS TO THE UNITED STATES: 12 WAYS TO LOCATE A BUYER*

Exporters in developing countries can use a variety of proven, yet often relatively inexpensive, methods to find a buyer in the U.S. market. As the world's largest market for consumer goods, the United States can offer numerous sales possibilities for exporters in developing countries. To take advantage of these opportunities, however, suppliers must know how to locate and contact the right buyers. U.S. buyers play a larger role in international business transactions than simply purchasing goods. They also often cooperate with producers in developing countries to adapt products for export, for instance

*By Richard R. Gesteland manager of a regional overseas buying office for a large U.S. chain, located in Italy. He opened a similar buying office in India several years ago, and prior to that carried out various overseas marketing assignments in Europe for U.S. export firms. He has written articles on export marketing and international bussiness for several U.S. business and economic journals.

by providing product specifications; giving design and styling guidance; offering training in quality control; and counselling on packaging, labelling and shipping. Successful market entry therefore depends to a great extent on finding the appropriate business partner. The discussion that follows focuses on how exporters of consumer durables and non-duarables in developing countries can effectively make such contacts.

Who are the Buyers?

What is meant by the term "buyer"? For exporters of consumer goods, three distinct types of buyers are of interest in the U.S. market:

1. Importers, trading companies and other merchant intermediaries that buy from manufacturers abroad and resell to U.S. retailers.
2. U.S. manufacturers looking for foreign suppliers of goods to complement their own lines.
3. U.S. retailers such as chain stores and large department stores that buy directly from overseas suppliers, rather than through middlemen.

The tactics for locating buyers discussed in the following section apply to all three types of buyers, except where noted to the contrary.

Tips on Finding a Buyer

Exporters in developing countries can use a numbers of different techniques to find buyers in the U.S. market. Many of these involue almost no expense at all—they consist basically of knowing what sources to contact and what type of information to request from them. Others entail more financial outlay, but they should be cost-effective if carried out the right way.

Each of the 12 techniques discussed below is a valid source of leads to potential customers, as each has been used with success by exporters around the world, although perhaps less often by those in developing countries—simply because not all such sources are well known.

1. The National Trade Promotion Agency: A valuable source of leads to potential U.S. buyers is the national trade promotion agency in the exporter's own country. In many cases the trade information service in this organization has built up inquiry files and contact lists to help prospective exporters find trading partners overseas. These lists are sometimes developed in conjunction with the country's national trade representation service abroad The trade promotion agency may have a special system for disseminating such trade inquiries to selected business firms in the country, or it may publish them in its general bulletin or newsletter.

A further source in a trade promotion agency is the published material available from the agency's trade information service. A would-be exporter should avidly read international trade publications, both general periodicals and those specialized in his particular branch or industry. Articles in daily, weekly and monthly business publications frequently give details about U.S. companies of potential interest to developing country exporters. In addition, the basic reference works in a trade information service usually include directories of foreign importers, which can likewise be a tool for locating trade contacts.

2 Chambers and Other Business Associations: Local chambers of commerce and trade associations are another source of leads on portential buyers. Some chambers in developing countries have a regular system for putting their members in touch with interested business partners overseas. They may do this through special publications or through direct contact with the relevant exporters. Certain chambers work hand in hand with their national trade promotion agency to disseminate such trade opportunities to the business community Interested exporters should get in touch with both of these organizations

to see what types of leads they receive and now they inform businessmen about them.

3. Official U.S. Offices Abroad: U.S. embassies and consulates located in developing countries from time to time receive inquiries from American firms looking for new suppliers. Exporters could contact these offices to see if any such requests are relevant to their line of business. In addition, the commercial section of the embassy often houses a library stocked with useful business periodicals and reference works that contain leads to potential customers. Some helpful directories of this type are *American Export Register* (Thomas Publishing. 1 Penn Plaza, N.Y., N.Y. 10001. U.S.A.); *Encyclopedia of Associations* (Gale Research, Book Tower, Detroit, Mich. 48226, U.S.A.); and *World Guide to Trade Associations* (K.G. Saur Verlag, Possenbacherstr 2b, Postfach 711C09, D-8000 Munich 71, Federal Republic of Germany).

4. International banks: In many developing countries international banks are another source of leads. Banks often receive trade inquiries from branches of their own organization in other countries and from corresponding banks abroad. It is in the bank's interest to refer such inquiries to potential suppliers, since this helps generate new business for the bank in letter-of-credit operations and trade financing.

5. Export Servicing Firms: It is likewise in the interest of freight forwarders, customs brokers, airlines and steamship companies to promote new business link-ups. Such service firms are in a position to refer trade leads picked up from their foreign contacts to local exporters. Many international airlines also maintain airfreight marketing offices designed to promote air cargo business. They too may be able to help find customers for an exporter's line of products. It would be advisable to double check the business standing of any such firms suggested, for example through the local bank's international network, before any transactions are initiated.

Key European Trade Fairs Popular with U.S. Buyers

Fashion Shows

Heimtextil (home furnishings)	Frankfurt
Pitti Uomo (menswear, accessories)	Florence
Campionaria (leatherwear, accessories)	Florence
Jewelry Show	Vicenza
Pitti Bimbo (children's wear)	Florence
Pitti Casual (sportswear)	Florence
Pitti Filati (yarns)	Florence
Ladies' Ready-to-wear	Paris
Sehm-Menswear	Paris
Men's Fashion Week, International Jeans Fair	Cologne
Micam/Moda Caizalura (footwear)	Milan
Igedo (women's ready to wear, lingerie, etc.)	Dusseldorf
Mipel (leather goods, accessories)	Milan
GDS Shoe Fair	Dusseldorf
Modit/Milano Vendemoda (women's ready-to-wear accessories)	Milan
Interstoff (fabrics)	Frankfurt

Hard Goods, General Merchandise Fairs

Macef (housewares, gifts)	Milan
Frankfurt International Fair (consumer goods)	Frankfurt
Mido (eyeglasses, sunglasses)	Milan
Ispo (sporting goods, active footwear)	Munich
Spoga (camping, garden, outdoor furniture)	Cologne
International Hardware Fair	Cologne
Toy Fair	Nuremberg
Partners for Progress	Berlin (West)

6. Port Authorities: Less well known sources of lead for names of potential buyers in the United States are the various port authorities in the country. Some examples are the Port Authority of New York and New Jersey (address: 1 World Trade Centre, New York. N.Y. 10048); South Carolina State Port Authority (P.O. Box 817, Charleston, S.C. 29402); and the Port of New Orleans Board of Commissioners (P.O. Box 60046, New Orleans, La. 70160). Such offices are also located at other entry points in the country. Since port authorities work closely with U.S. importers, they are in a position to supply useful suggestions on possible buyers.

7. The AAEI: Another potential source of leads for developing country exporters is the American Association of Exporters and Importers (AAEI). The AAEI will consider publishing notices in its journal, called *International Trade*, from foreign manufacturers offering specific products for sale in the United States. The Association can be contacted for further information at 11 West 42nd Street, New York, N.Y. 10036.

A Selected List of Large U.S. Retail Concerns with Numerous Buying Offices Abroad

A. Chain Stores:

1. Sears Roebuck and Co.
   Sears Tower
   Chicago, Ill, 60684
2. Montgomery Ward and Co., Inc.
   Montgomery Ward Plaza
   Chicago, Ill, 60671
3. J.C. Penney Co.
   1301 Ave. of the Americas
   New York, N.Y. 10019
4. K-Mart
   3100 W. Big Beaver
   Troy, Mich. 48084

B. Department Stores:

1. R.H. Macy and Co., Inc.
   Broadway and 34th Street
   New York, N.Y. 10001
2. Allied Stores Corp.
   1114 Ave. of the Americas
   New York, N.Y. 10036
3. Associated Dry Goods Corp.
   417 5th Ave.
   New York, N.Y. 10016
4. Marshall Field and Co.
   111 North State St.
   Chicago, Ill, 60690
5. May Department Stores Co.
   611 Olive Street
   St. Louis, Mo, 63101
6. Gimbel Bros. Inc.
   Gimbel Corp. Buying Offices
   c/o Mutual Buying Office
   11 W. 42nd Street
   New York, N.Y. 10036

7. Associated Merchandising Corporation
1440 Broadway
New York, N.Y. 10018
(Associated Merchandising Corporation is the overseas buying organization for many well known stores such as Bloomingdale's.)

---

8. Marketing Consultants: An exporter in a developing country may decide to employ a marketing consultant to handle market research and locate buyers. This will involve greater expense than the other techniques already reviewed, but the results may justify the cost. *Bradford's Directory of Marketing Research Agencies and Management Consultants* (published by Bradford's Directory of Marketing Agencies, Box 276, Fairfax, Va. 220 0, U.S.A.) would be useful to locate the names of appropriate consultants. Major U.S. Universities also sometimes offer help in selecting a consultant of this type. One example is Georgetown University's National Center for Export-Import Studies in Washington, D.C (address: 37th and O Streets, N.W., Washington, D.C. 20057, U.S.A.).

9. International Trade Fairs: Given the critical importance of finding the right buyer, an exporter in a developing country may prefer to seek one out directly. If he has the funds available to do so, an efficient way for him to do this might be to attend trade fairs and exhibitions abroad. Given the costs involved in participating in foreign fairs, exporters should carefully select the ones they exhibit in.

Specialized trade fairs are organized in most of the developing regions. The advantages of regional fairs held in developing countries are two:

1. the cost and effort required to set up a booth are relatively modest and
2. most of the visiting foreign buyers are by definition seeking suppliers in that region. A regional trade show is thus a good stepping-stone to exporting, not only for selling to other countries in the region but also for meeting buyers from outside the area.

Another measure, involving greater expense and effort, is participation in major European international trade fairs. The Federal Republic of Germany, France, the United Kingdom and Italy, for emample, all organize major seasonal fashion and general merchandise shows that are attended by hundreds of U.S. importers and retail buyers. Because of the concentration of visiting U.S. buyers, these major European fairs are a very effective way to meet customers. A developing country exporter may set up a booth on his own, jointly with other exporters or together with a sponsoring organization, such as the national trade promotion organization. Even though a U.S. buyer of denim jeans may be attending a show in Milan to review European collections, for example, he or she well certainly be prepared to look at a tastefully presented line of jeans from a developing country as well.

The major European trade fairs listed on page 16 were selected because they are (1) well attended by U.S. buyers and (2) show merchandise of great interest to developing country exporters of consumer goods. [The Partners for Progress fair in Berlin (West), one of those listed, is a particularly important show for developing country exporters. For further information contact AMK, Messedamm 22, 1000 Berlin (West) 19.]

The major advantage of participating in fairs outside the United States is that the U.S. buyers attending them are purposely looking for foreign suppliers. Hence the exporter has a good chance of finding a customer. Another tactic, however, is to attend trade shows in the United States. Although in some cases only a fraction of the buyers in attendance may be interested in overseas suppliers, the total number of visitors may be quite large, thereby offering the possibility for many useful contacts. An up-to-date list of fairs and exhibitions should be available at any U.S. embassy.

10. Piggybacking: Another tactic, very little used, for making contact with potential customers is "piggybacking." Under this arrangement, a potential exporter identifies a

Specimen Letter for an Article of Clothing

Best Garments Co.
Capital City
Agraria

13 September 1984

Federal Apparel Imports
Attn: Mr. Sam Spade
1776 Independence Blvd.
Los Angeles, Co. 90012
U.S.A.

Dear Mr. Spade:

This letter is to introduce Best Garments, one of my country's top knit shirt manufacturers. I was unable to contact you during your recent buying trip to Agraria, and wish to take this opportunity to provide you with important details regarding our production.

Our speciality is 100 per cent cotton men's polo shirts in 40s yarn, which we are exporting to several industrialized countries. We have just installed the most modern shrinkage-control equipment available on the world market, and hence can guarantee you maximum residual shrinkage of 3 per cent when laundered "Wash Warm, Dry Cool."

I enclose a copy of a recent letter from our largest customer in East Urbania, testifying to our quality and reliability as suppliers. Best Garments can ship you up to 5,000 knit shirts per month over the next six months. After that our five new circular knitting machines and 22 new overlock machines will enable us to double our available capacity.

Attached is a descriptive brochure and a price list in U.S. dollars, CIF Los Angeles. We are eager to send you a sample of shirts from our current collection, in U.S. sizos. Or you may send us a photo, sketch or reference sample from which we will develop a counter-sample for you.

I look forward to seeing you at the next NAMSB show in New York.

Sincerely,

X Zelda
Vice-President, Marketing

successful exporter in his country of a related but noncompeting product. He makes an agreement with the experienced exporter, under which his partner will add the new product to his own line of exports, thereby introducing the new goods to the buyers that he is already dealing with possible partners can be suggested by the national trade promotion agency, local changer of commerce and the relevant trade association, as well as by banks and freight forwarders. In addition, governments often publicize achievement awards to outstanding exporters, who could be potential piggyback partners.

A manufacturer of leather handbags in South America, for example, might approach a firm in his own country successfully exporting footwear to the United States. Or an Egyptian producer of woven sports shirts in Cairo might join forces with a successful exporter of T-shirts in Alexandria. This can be a low-cost and effective export marketing tactic, provided that the new exporter carefully checks the credentials of his prospective piggyback partner.

11. Advertisements: Firms in developing countries interested in subcontracting (assembly) work for U S. customers may be able to find such opportunities by placing advertisements in specialized American trade journals and newspapers. Potential customers for such ads would be not only importers and major retail chains but also U.S. manufacturers wishing to add an import product to their own domestically produced product line.

Typical products that U.S. firms arrange to have assembled abroad are consumer electronic articles and "cut-make-trim" appared (*i.e.*, garments produced from fabric and components supplied by the customer). The U.S. firm ships all parts and components to the foreign subcontractor, who in turn sends back the completely assembled product, be it a pocket calculator or a dress shirt. If the product qualifies under item 807 of the Tariff Schedules of the United States, the duty is assessed only on the value added abroad by the assembly work. In practice, the type of assembly contracting foreseen under this provision is usually undertaken only by firms operating in Mexico and the Central American region because the cost of shipping the parts and components to more distant locations is high).

12. Overseas resident buying offices: The discussion so far has focused on ways for an exporter to find a buyer located in the United States. There is, however, a major channel of contact frequently overlooked by exporters in developing countries. This is the network of overseas resident buying offices maintained by large chain stores and department stores in the United States.

Exporters in developing countries are often unaware that U.S. retail buyers do not passively wait to be approached by hopeful suppliers. Instead they actively scout out new products and new resources all over the world. For this reason the major U.S. retail concerns have established regional buying offices abroad, expressly to seek out and develop new suppliers of all types of consumer goods.

Resident buying offices tend to be concentrated in areas of the world that are already major suppliers to the U.S. market. In Asia, for example, these offices are clustered in Japan, Hong Kong, China (Taiwan Province), the Republic of Korea and Singapore, and also exist to a more limited extent in Thailand, India and Sri Lanka. In Latin America buying offices are less common, but some are located in Brazil, Colombia and Mexico.

Africa and the Middle East are principally served by resident buying offices located in Europe. Resident buyers in Italy and Spain are typically charged with coverage of Africa and West Asia. There is, for example, a large cluster of regional buying offices in Florence, Italy. African and West Asian exporters may write to the National Association of Italian Buying Offices for a complete listing of such offices located in Italy: Associazione Nazionale Italiana Buying Offices (ANIBO), Via Tornabuoni 16, 50123 Florence, Italy.

Exporters in developing countries can get in touch with the U.S. buying offices nearest them in three ways:

1. Inquire with the commercial officer at the nearest U.S. embassy or consulate.

2. Consult Directory of American Firms Operating in Foreign Countries (published by World Trade Academy Press Inc., 50 E. 42nd Street, New York, N.Y. 10017, U.S A.).

3. Write major retailers in the United States, asking for the address and contact person of their nearest overseas buying office.

A partial listing of large U.S. retail concerns with numerous buying offices abroad is given in the box on page 97 (the list is not exhaustive; other firms may also be of interest for particular lines of goods).

It is important for exporters in developing countries to note that although these retailers are very large, the segmentation of the U.S. consumer goods market is such that these stores buy from medium-size and even small manufacturers, as well as larger suppliers. Especially in fashion merchandise such as appared, footwear and accessories, style changes are frequent and production runs are relatively short. Retailers and importers buy such goods from overseas factories with as few as a dozen employees. Large buyers combine the production capacity of many small manufacturers as needed to cover demand. (When they do so, of course. they must assure that goods of a standard quality are produced by each supplier). So even a small producer need not hesitate to try to enter the U.S. market through this channel.

Contact with a customer of this type will be caster in cases where the U.S. retailer maintains a local buying agent in the exporter's country. When such agents exist. their names and addresses are available from the regional office or directly from the retail concern's U.S. headquarters office.

Specimen Letter for a Light Manufactured Item

Wizard Wood Turnings Works
1601 West State St.
Ruralia
29 July 1984

American Retail Co.
Attn: Ms. Jane Q. Smith
1984 Broadway
New York, N.Y. 10001
U.S.A.

Dear Ms. Smith:

It was indeed a pleasure meeting you at the 100th Annual World Fair of Wood Turnings. We have been manufacturing wood turnings since 1946 and currently produce 26,000 per week. Our factory in Ruralia has 13 of the latest machines for this purpose and employs 198 workers. We are now installing seven new pieces of equipment that will double our capacity by September. Our firm is a 100 per cent Ruralian-owned private company.

You will recall that you were especially impressed with our octagonal wood turnings at the Fair. I am enclosing a 30-page colour catalogue showing the Wizard Wood Turnings Works' octagonal product in operation from every angle. (Please note the detailed spec sheet attached). We will be happy to rush you a sample via airfreight. Please telex us in this regard.

We presently export the octagonal item to 16 markets, of which Urbania is the largest. In 1983 we sold a total of US$ 2.5 million worth of the octagonal and square items abroad, some 43 per cent of our annual production.

The attached quotation sheet gives our 1984 prices in US dollars, CIF New York, valid through the calendar year. (Please note the special discount for rectangular wood turnings with or without the screw-on attachment).

I will be in New York in September. Would the week of the 24th be convenient for a meeting to discuss the delivery situation?

Sincerely yours,
Waldo Burnhem
Export Director

Prospective exporters in developing countries would be well advised to establish contact with some of these buying offices and agents. Although the organization and functions of resident buying offices vary from one company to another, an office of this type generally carries out the following important tasks:

Survey markets in the region.
Screen potential suppliers.
Select products.
Develop new products with selected suppliers.

Provide guidance on labelling, ticketing (*i.e.*, attaching pre-printed retail price tickets), packaging, carton marketing and shipping of the merchandise.

II

GENERAL TERMS AND CONDITIONS—AN IMPORTANT ELEMENT IN FOREIGN TRADE TRANSACTIONS*

Exporters and importers too often overlook the general terms and conditions that govern their overseas business operations. Exporters and importers often do not give sufficient attention to the "general terms and conditions" governing their international trade transactions. Yet these terms and conditions, which are usually given in small print on the back of the sales offer or acceptance form, and subsequently become part of the sales contract, can have substantial financial consequences for the two parties concerned. "General terms and conditions" are the basic set of provisions that determines the rights and obligations of the buyer and the seller on such matters as the quality and quantity of the goods to be supplied, the packing

*This article is based on a paper that Branko Vukmir recently prepared for ITC on the legal aspects of general terms and conditions in international trade contracts. Mr. Vukmir teaches and practices law in Zagreb, Yugoslavia. He has served as a consultant on the legal aspects of foreign trade with various ITC technical cooperation projects in developing countries.

and marketing of those goods, pre-shipment inspection, shipping documents, means of delivery, transfer of risk, acceptance of the goods, guarantees, price, payment. recourse in the event of nonperformance of the contract and the procedure for settling claims. The conditions governing these subjects can involve financial responsibility for the parties to the transaction. New exporters and importers in developing countries in particular may not be aware of the existence of these conditions or of their significance for trading operations. They should therefore familiarize themselves with the purpose and content of such conditions, as well as with the way in which they are drawn up and applied.

The Form of General Terms and Conditions

Large companies in industrialized countries that trade internationally on a regular basis have usually laid down a standard set of general terms and conditions for their own use. These conditions are printed on the back of their offer and acceptance forms. This text, which generally covers a dozen or more provisions under different headings, gives in detail the obligations of the buyer and the seller on the range of subjects governed by the sales contract. The terms and conditions spelled out by the firm are those that it wishes to have accepted by its prospective trading partners.

Exporters and importers in developing countries, particularly small, new firms just entering foreign trade, often have not drawn up their own set of general terms and conditions. Instead they may simply accept those presented to them by the foreign buyer or seller, whichever the case may be, perhaps without reading through them carefully. In some situations they may not even be aware that the foreign business partner has submitted his terms and conditions to them as the basis for the contract, since these provisions are usually not very noticeable: They are generally printed on the back of the buyer's or supplier's standard forms, in small type, and sometimes in a light colour of ink. When such clauses are accepted by the second party, either explicitly or tacitly, they bind that party to the conditions concerned. If a trader in a developing country, for example, unknowingly agrees to terms that are not acceptable to him, he may be placed in an unfavourable trading position later on. Such provisions should therefore be studied carefully. Exporters and importers in developing countries would be well advised to establish their own set of general terms and conditions as a basis for their overseas transactions, which they can refer to when examining the other party's proposed conditions and apply as necessary.

When Conflicts in Conditions Arise

When the terms and conditions of the two parties differ—which is not infrequent since there is no standard formal for these provisions the two parties should discuss these differences and come to an agreement upon terms that are suitable and reasonable for both. The extent to which a small, new exporter in a developing country can attempt to have his terms accepted by his foreign business partner will depend for a large part upon his commercial bargaining strength vis-a-vis the other party. He cannot expect to impose all of his own terms and conditions on his overseas partner if the other firm is a large trader who can readily find clients or suppliers elsewhere. However even a small company should bring any difficulties it foresees in the proposed terms to the attention of the other party, as it is in the interest of both trading partners that the conditions be mutually satisfactory.

In practice, for example, when an importer in a developing country receives an offer from a foreign supplier, and the offer includes a set of general terms and conditions, the importer should go through these terms against the set of conditions that he has drawn up for his own use. If there are differences or conflicts between the two, he could convey his acceptance of the other party's terms, subject to a modification of the specific terms and conditions that he considers unacceptable. This approach would be more practical and effective than simply sending his entire set of conditions to the potential supplier, who may consider the importer's terms as one-sided and may not therefore regard the proposed business transaction as worthwhile, particularly if the order is small. By identifying a few key differences to be discussed, on the other hand, the importer may be able to gain acceptance for his terms and thereby ensure that his interests are protected.

The same approach could be used by a small exporter in a developing country. If his prospective buyer abroad sends him a set of general conditions with his order, the exporter could specify in his confirmation letter that he would like for certain additional or amended clauses to be considered as conditions governing the transaction. The exporter's own general terms and conditions could serve as a reference for his review of the clauses, and he could note the main provisions to be discussed in a covering letter with the confirmation of his offer.

Contents of General Conditions

An exporter or an importer in a developing country who is drawing up a set of general conditions could take as examples the conditions established by other companies trading internationally. But these should serve only as a source of ideas, as each company requires its own particular set of conditions adapted to its production and trading situation and to any local regulations or laws that may be relevant. The conditions will vary, for instance, depending on the type of product being traded (for instance, whether it is a commodity or heavy equipment); the size of the trader's foreign business operations, and consequently his bargaining position in the market; and the type of trading operation concerned (*e.g.*, a long-term versus a short-term transaction).

An example of what a set of general terms and conditions might cover is given on pages 117 to 127. The example is not intended to serve as a "model" but rather to give an indication of what such conditions could contain. Certain assumptions have been made in the example, which might or might not apply to an actual case, *i.e.*, that the country in which the company is located has instituted foreign exchange controls and that all imports pass through a central freight office. The related provisions in the general terms and conditions therefore reflect hypothetical national laws on these matters. Some of the provisions in the example are taken from a proposed international treaty, the UN Convention on Contracts for the International Sale of Goods, adopted in Vienna in 1980 by various governments and now open for ratification. (When and if the convention is ratified by the required number of states and comes into force, it will not replace the need for general terms and conditions in international sales transactions, as general conditions will continue to be necessary to regulate specific business dealings between two parties).

The example of general terms and conditions given here reflects for a large part the interests of the buyer. In an actual business transaction the buyer might therefore need to make compromises on some of these points in order to obtain the agreement of the seller on the conditions to govern the transaction. This process of discussing conflicting or differing terms and conditions between the two parties is a frequent element in business negotiations, as discussed above.

Explanation of the Example

The provisions in the example are largely self-explanatory. However the discussion below on individual points may help to explain the reasoning behind some of the clauses in the example and to clarify various legal points in the text.

1. Which conditions to apply. When the buyer and the seller send their own general conditions to each other, either with the offer or with the acceptance, the problem of which of these two sets of conditions is to be considered as valid may arise. In point 1. of the example, an attempt has been made to exclude any general conditions other than those of the buyer, unless the other conditions have been explicitly accepted by the

buyer. However, such a provision may not in itself automatically exclude general conditions proposed by the other party, particularly if the other set of conditions has a similar provision. Buyers should therefore pay attention in each case to the conditions of the other party and exclude them explicitly if a conflict between the two may occur.

2. Conclusion of the contract: The basic issue here is the question of who controls the conclusion of the contract-the buyer or the seller. The party whose decision or action is necessary to make the contract valid is the one who controls its conclusion.

3. Assignment: Under this provision, the buyer has reserved the power of assignment for himself, as he did for the conclusion of the contract, discussed above. Assignment refers to the transfer of the rights and obligations under the contract to a third party.

4. Pre-shipment inspection: A few developing countries require that a special certificate of quality and quantity, sometimes called a "Clean Report of Findings," be issued by a controlling agency prior to delivery of the goods, and, as a rule, prior to the loading of the goods on the vessel. Many buyers in developing countries confuse the issuance of this document with acceptance of the goods. Such confusion can adversely affect the buyer's contractual rights. If the issuance of a "Clean Report of Findings" were considered as an "acceptance," the buyer would lose his rights to examine the goods upon arrival and the right to reject them at that point if they did not correspond to the contractual conditions. This would be contrary to the purpose for which the Clean Report was issued. Such documents should be considered only as certificates of quality and quantity rather than as representing "acceptance" by the buyer.

5. and 6. Quantity and quality: Both provisions refer to "price reduction" if the goods do not conform to the quality and/or quantity specified in the contract. This is traditional civil

law recourse that is included in the UN Convention on Contracts for the International Sale of Goods, in spite of the fact it is not provided for in countries with a "common law" legal system. Price reduction is a practical means in international trade to get recourse when the goods do not conform to the order. They are thus left with the buyer rather than being shipped back to the seller.

7. Delivery: Due to various exchange restrictions, many developing countries face the problem of opening a letter of credit (L/C) within the time specified in the sales contract. If the opening of the letter of credit is a condition for the entry into force of the contract, the parties do not know whether they have a contract or not, until the buyer opens the L/C. If the L/C is not opened on time, the seller can, if he so wishes, simply disassociate himself from the transaction. It would, therefore, be more advisable to tie the opening of the L/C with the delivery terms, rather than with the validity of the contract. The contract would then enter into force when signed and when other conditions were fulfilled. The opening of the L/C would have an influence only on the delivery terms, and may be on the price, if the parties so agree.

Penalties or liquidated damages are usual sanctions for late deliveries. Liquidated damages are considered more appropriate for international trade than penalties because they are fixed in advance regardless of the actual damage suffered. For this reason they are given in the example. However, they should not be confused with sanctions for nonfulfillment of the contract. If the delivery does not take place within the time period provided for in the contract, the seller must pay the agreed liquidated damages. But if the seller is late even after that time, the buyer has other means of recourse at his disposal, including termination of the contract and the claiming of damages for breach of contract. In other words, liquidated damages are not to be considered as full compensation for nonfulfillment of the entire contract—they are compensation only for the specific failure provided in the contract and not for breach of other conditions.

8. Acceptance: This provision is closely related to the pre-shipment inspections provision (clause 4), but it carries the point of conformity of the goods with the contract even further by stating that the goods shall be considered to have been accepted only when the buyer has had a reasonable opportunity to inspect them after they have been delivered to him. That means that the buyer is entitled to examine the goods after the sea voyage is completed and when he has a "reasonable opportunity" to do so. Moreover, the liability of the seller remains effective for latent defects even after the acceptance of the goods.

9. Packing and marking: It is clear that the packing and marking of goods is the responsibility of the seller. The question is only what standards of packing and marking the seller should apply. In the example, the standards are specified as being those suitable for the overseas transport of the type of goods in question, and the markings should remain readable until the buyer has received the goods.

10. Transfer of risk: Part of this provision is connected with acceptance (see point 8. above), because the risk connected with delivering the goods reverts to the seller even if it has already passed to the buyer, if the goods are rejected at any time during the transaction. Together with the risk, the property also reverts to the seller in such cases, thereby relieving the buyer of the return cost and other problems if the goods delivered are not in accordance with the contract.

11., 12. and 13. Prices, payment and shipping documents: Certain provisions in these three clauses have been based on hypothetical exchange control provisions that exist in the imaginary country concerned, but they may be applicable in similar situations when import licenses have strict expiry terms.

14. Guarantées and warranties: The definition of "conformity," like the rest of the clause on this subject, has been basically taken from the UN convention on the sale of goods, referred to above. A change has been introduced in the last section, where it is stated that the guarantee for conformity extends for 12 months "after acceptance" and not "after taking over" as provided in the UN convention. It is thought that, for buyers, the time of acceptance is more favourable than the time of taking over (which is relevant for the passing of risk), because it postpones the period during which guarantees begin to take effect and thus allows for a longer guarantee period.

15. Remedies: Some "remedies, "or means of legal redress against loss of or damage to the goods, are contained in earlier clauses of the example (for instance 5, 6 and 7). The basic remedy is a request for the cover of damages. An additional remedy is repudiation of the contract if the consequences of the breach are serious and the nonperformance is fundamental. The seller has the possibility, if the buyer so agrees, to reimburse the buyer at his own expense for any failure in his performance of the contract, even after he has delivered the goods, but the buyer is not obliged to give the seller this opportunity.

Additional remedies may be added, such as the right of the buyer to procure goods from other sources on the risk and at the expense of the buyer or to terminate the right of the seller to proceed with part of the contract.

16. Exemptions: Again, the UN convention war the basis for this clause. It Is considered that current differences in national legal systems, with their traditional concepts of "force majeure" or "frustration", make such terms difficult to apply in international trade transactions, in which more understanding and flexibility is expected for events beyond the control of the parties than in domestic trade. Therefore, new concepts have been entering this area for some time, and the UN convention on the sale of goods is a continuation of this process. However, certain provisions in the UN convention that favour

the seller have been left out of this example, for instance, the right to claim exemption due to nonperformance by third persons engaged by the seller.

17. Third-party claims: This clause is of relevance in cases where the goods sold infringe upon some patent or other intellectual property rights of third parties. In such cases the buyer can unexpectedly be sued by a third party, and he may wish to have coverage for such a contingency in his purchase contract.

18. Settlement of disputes and applicable law: The wording of this clause follows the wording recommended by the arbitration rules of the UN Commission on International Trade Law (UNCITRAL). In the example, these rules have been used instead of the arbitration rules of the International Chamber of Commerce (ICC), which are often found in international trade contracts, UNCITRAL, rules of arbitration are employed for situations of ad hoc arbitration, that is, arbitration not conducted by an institution such as the ICC but rather by arbitrators selected by the parties themselves. If the parties wish, they may change the appointing, authority, the number of arbitrators, the place of arbitration, the language used in the proceedings and the applicable law. In the example, the provision on dispute settlement gives particular consideration to the interests of the buyer.

Give advice on quality control.

Make payment to the supplier.

Handle merchandise claims, if any.

Contacting the Buyer

When a U.S. buyer has been located, the most professional way for the exporter to contact him is through a merchandise offer letter. The offer letter should be written in simple, clear English —unless there is a good reason to believe that correspondence in another language is acceptable. It should be typed neatly and legibly on the exporter's business letterhead. Usually one to two pages are enough to cover the subject.

The six principal elements of a good offer letter are the following:

1. A description of the manufacturer's business: the size of his production facility, the types of equipment in his plant, his production capacity and general background on his business operations.
2. Details on his products a description of it, specifiations where necessary, and the inclusion in the letter of a product catalogue, brochure or photo of the article, where appropriate.
3. Background on the firm's export experience: a brief statement about which markets and to what type of customer the firm is already exporting, with a rough idea of the volume of these sales in units or dollars: new exporters should explain why they would be a good supplier.
4. Information concerning samples: the exporter should offer to send a sample of his product upon the buyer's request and should mention if the product is available immediately.
5. Reference to a personal visit: the letter should explain under what circumstances the exporter may be able to visit the buyer. possibly carrying reference samples.
6. Details on prices, delivery and terms: the exporter should quote prices CIF U.S. when corresponding with a buyer in the United States. For an offer to an overseas resident buying office in his region, an exporter can quote prices either CIF or FOB port of export, or both. He should indicate what the delivery delay is and the financial terms of his offer. Letter of credit payment is the normal form of financial arrangement at the beginning of a business relationship.

Specimen Letter for a Processed Food Product

Southern Spices Ltd.
Liberation Plaza, 10
Ruralia
21 August 1184

U.S. Food Products, Inc.
Attn: Mr. John Jones
1 North Michigan Avenue
Chicago, III, 606000
U.S.A.

Dear Mr. Jones:

We have just learned from the Ruralian Trade Development Agency that your company is seeking a reliable supplier of pickled capers and carob powder· The RTDA informed us that you require the capers in four-ounce glass jars, 12 jars to a carton, and carob powder in 10-ounce cans.

Our firm produces 16 metric tons of carob powder per year, exported mainly to Exurbian food distributors and large retailers. Our factory was built in 1980 and currently employs 45 workers.

Southern Spices Ltd. specializes in pickled capers, of which we ship some 140,000 cases annually to 13 different countries. We normally pack in 250-gram jars, but with a minimum order of 5,000 cases we can also supply you in four-ounce glass jars with screw top lids and four-colour labels.

The attached literature provides complete product specifications and price information. Our terms are confirmed, irrevocable letter of credit at sight.

We have airfreighted you a full range of carod powder and caper samples in our normal export packing Of course we would supply the correct labels for your market upon receipt of complete labelling information from you.

Many thanks for your kind inqury. We look forward to becoming your regular supplier of fine quality foods.

Yours sincerely,

Yosef Wan
General Manager

(See the boxes on pages 100, 104 and at right for specimen offer letters for an article of clothing a light manufactured item and processed food).

If the exporter has not received a reply from the buyer after four to six weeks, he may wish to send a polite follow-up letter, attaching a copy of the original offer. Communication by telex or telephone with the prospective buyer is generally advisable only *after* the buyer has responded to the exporter's initial offer.

Following up a Favourable Response

A positive reply should be followed up immediately. The exporter should first answer any questions asked by the buyer. Then he should send any further literature or samples needed and suggest arrangements for a meeting, where appropriate.

Conclusion

A wide variety of proven ways can be used to locate and contract a U.S. buyer. But the buyer remains only a potential customer until the sale is made. Furthermore, he does not become a *repeat* customer unless the first sales contract is properly fulfilled. Finding a buyer is therefore only the first step in successfully exporting to the United States, but it is a very important and necessary one that cannot be overlooked.

APPENDIX

Example: General Terms and Conditions of Purchase

1. General

All contracts and agreements of sale (hereafter referred to as "contracts") concluded on the basis of this indent (order) are subject to these general terms and conditions of purchase unless the buyer specifically agrees to modify them in writing.

Other general terms and conditions that may be attached to the seller's offers and/or acceptances of orders and/or other quotations are made part of the contract only if specifically accepted in writing by the buyer.

2. Conclusion of the Contract

A contract shall be considered as concluded either when a contract document is signed by the buyer and seller, or, if the parties do not intend to sign such a document, when the seller's offer has been accepted in writing by the buyer.

3. Assignment

The seller is not allowed to assign the contract in whole or in part or to assign any of his rights or obligations under the contract without the prior written consent of the buyer.

4. Pre-shipment Inspection

In all cases where pre-shipment inspection for quality, quantity and price has been agreed upon or when it is mandatory, the seller shall send a notice to the inspection agency at least ten days before the expected date of shipment with precise information on where and when such inspection may be performed. Such a notice shall be accompanied by the relative proforma invoice, photocopies of the letter of credit (where applicable), the purchase contract and any other document relevant for the purposes of inspection.

The cost of presentation of the goods for inspection, as well as the cost of inspection, unpacking, repacking, handling of the goods etc. shall be borne by the seller. The seller accepts that, unless a "Clean Report of Findings" is issued by the inspecting agency in respect of the inspected goods, no payment shall be made for such imports, even if other documents are in order and irrespective of the agreed mode of payment. A "Non-negotiable Report of Findings" may be issued if the inspection reveals discrepancies between the goods and the terms of the contract. Pre-shipment inspection is not to be considered as acceptance of the inspected goods, and the issuance of a "Clean Report of Findings" shall not relieve the seller of any of his contractual obligations to the buyer. The buyer always reserves the right to examine the goods upon delivery and to reject them if they are found to be in nonconformance with the contract.

5. Quantity

The quantity of goods delivered by the seller must be conformity with the contract.

If the seller delivers a quantity of goods less than that in the contract, the buyer may reject them. But if the goods are accepted as delivered, the buyer shall pay for the accepted quantity at the contract rates. If the seller delivers a quantity of goods larger than that he has contracted to sell, the buyer may accept the goods included in the contract and reject the rest, or he may reject the whole. But if he accepts them. he shall pay for them at the contract rates. If the seller delivers contracted goods mixed with goods of a different description not included in the contract, the buyer may accept the goods that are in accordance with the contract and reject the rest, or he may reject the whole.

If the goods are rejected fully or partially due to nonconformity in quantity, the buyer is always entitled to claim damages or reduce the price, whichever may be relevant.

6. Quality

The quality of the goods delivered by the seller must be in conformity with the contract. If there are no special contract. If there are no special contractual provisions concerning the quality of goods to be delivered, it is understood that all goods shall be new and unused standard products suitable in all respects for their intended purpose. Spare parts should be identical to original parts.

If the quality of the goods does not conform with the contract, and regardless of whether the price has already been paid, the buyer may either reduce the price or claim damages and maintain the goods, or reject the goods repudiate the contract and claim damages.

If the buyer claims a reduction in price, such a reduction should correspond to the difference between the value of the goods at the time of delivery to the buyer and the value they would have had at the same time, had they been in conformity with the contract.

If the seller, in deliveries by stated installments, makes defective deliveries in respect of one or more installments, the buyer may treat such a breach as a repudiation of the whole contract, or may reduce the price or claim damages without repudiating the whole contract.

7. Delivery

Unless otherwise provided in the contract, when letter of credit payment is involved, the delivery time period shall start on the date when the seller receives the first notification of the issuing, advising or confirming bank (as the case may be) of the opening of the letter of credit. In contracts where other modes of payment are provided for the parties shall agree on the time when delivery terms shall start.

Failure to deliver within the time limit specified in the contract shall, in addition to other liabilities of the seller, entitle the buyer to impose a sum of 1 % (one per cent) of the contract price of the goods as liquidated damages sand not as a penalty) for every week or part thereof of delay and to reduce the price of such goods accordingly. The total amount of liquidated damages shall not be more than 20 % (twenty per cent) of the total value of the contracted goods. But as soon as such an amount is reached, the buyer may repudiate the contract, claim the total liquidated damages for delay and claim further damages for breach of contract.

If the seller does not deliver within the time period provided in the contract, or within the extended time as may be agreed by the buyer, the buyer is entitled to reject the goods without offering another delivery term, unless otherwise explicitly provided in the contract. However, if the delay is negligible, the buyer is not entitled to reject the goods but may claim liquidated damages for late delivery.

Unless otherwise agreed, the buyer is not obliged to accept delivery of the goods by installments.

If the seller neglects to deliver as contracted, the buyer may ask for damages that may be ascertained as the difference between the contract price and the market price at the time(s) the goods ought to have been delivered.

8. Acceptance

When the goods are delivered to the buyer in accordance with the contract, the buyer is not deemed to have accepted them unless and untill he has had a reasonable opportunity to examine them for the purpose of ascertaining whether they are in conformity with the contract. As a rule, and unless otherwise agreed, such a reasonable opportunity arises within as short a time as is practicable after the goods have arrived at the buyer's premises.

The buyer is considered to have accepted the goods when he declares to the seller that he has accepted them or when the goods have been delivered to him and, after a lapse of a reasonable time, he retains the goods without declaring to the seller that he has rejected them. The seller shall nevertheless remain responsible for all latent defects and/or guaranteed properties of the goods as provided in the contract, irrespective of the acceptance upon delivery. The seller shall remain responsible after acceptance in particular for the proper functioning of all machinery, apparatuses, instruments, equipment and goods until the expiration of the respective guarantee period. If the goods are rejected because they do not conform to the contract, the buyer shall, within a reasonable time, declare so to the seller. It is then the seller's duty to provide for their return at his expense and risk. If the goods are rejected, the contract is considered as repudiated.

9. Packing and Marking

The goods must be securely and adequately packed and/or protected in order to prevent damage and preserve them in overseas transit to the buyer. Storage must be arranged for in accordance with the provisions of the contract. If there are no special provisions in the contract concerning packaging, the goods should be packed in the manner usual for overseas transport of such goods.

All packages should be clearly marked in accordance with the contract. All packages the exceed one ton must be stenciled accurately to show the gross weight of each such package. Invoices must show the total net and gross metric weights of each package, together with an adequate description of the contents of each package.

All markings on packages must be such that they remain clearly readable until the end of transit and until the receipt of the goods by the buyer.

All losses and/or damage resulting from inadequate packaging inadequate protection or inadequate marking shall be borne by the seller.

10. Transfer of Risk

Unless otherwise agreed between the parties, the risk passes to the buyer when the goods are handed over to the first carrier for transmission to the buyer in accordance with the contract, provided the goods are clearly identified with the contract. If not otherwise specifically provided in the contract, trade terms used in the contract shall be interpreted in accordance with

"Incoterms" (the standard definitions and abbreviations for a list of terms commonly used in international trade, issued by the International Chamber of Commerce in Paris).

If the goods are rejected due to nonconformity with the contract or to unacceptable packing, risk and property shall revert to the seller until the situation has been remedied or the goods have been accepted.

If the seller is not bound to effect transport insurance, he must, at the buyer's request, provide all available information necessary to enable the buyer to arrange for such insurance.

11. Prices

Unless provided otherwise in the contract, all prices are considered firm and cover the costs of packaging, marking, protection and similar expenditures.

All expenses such as customs, taxes, bank charges, dues etc. in the country of origin or of the seller shall be borne by the seller, and, unless provided otherwise, all these expenses in the buyer's country shall be borne by the buyer.

12. Payment

Payment(s) shall be made within the time period, at the place and in the manner provided in the contract.

If payment(s) is to be made through the opening of a letter of credit (L/C), the L/C shall indicate also the expiry date of the relative import license. The seller is obliged to complete the shipment(s) up to the final destination covered by the import license, or to notify immediately upon receipt of the first advice of the L/C that he will not be able to complete the shipment(s) before such date(s).

The seller takes note of the fact that L/Cs will not be extended unless the relevant import license has also been revalidated, and unless a "Clean Report of Findings" is presented.

All payment(s) through the L/C may be effected only against delivery of the agreed shipping documents. All bills of lading presented to the banks must indicate the name and address of the importer and his bankers.

If the contract does not provid otherwise, the buyer shall bear the bank charges only of the bank in his own country and not of foreign banks.

13. Documents and Shipping

The seller is obliged to send to the buyer a teletransmitted shipping advice prior to obtaining the on-board bill of lading (B/L), containing the following information: contract number, port of loading, brief description of the goods, invoice amount of shipment, name of the vessel, estimated time of departure (ETD) and estimated time of arrival (ETA). The number of the B/L should be sent as soon as obtained.

At least one set of all documents related to the goods, whether negotiable or nonnegotiable, such as bills of lading, invoices, packing lists, insurance certificates, the certificate of origin and other transport documents should be airmailed by the seller to the buyer immediately after shipment in order to expedite customs procedures or for other contractual purposes. Delays in complying with the above shall entitle the buyer to claim compensation in case of damages occurred due to such noncompliance.

If the seller has handed over documents before the agreed time, he may, up to that time, correct any lack of conformity in the documents, if the exercise of this right does not cause the buyer unreasonable inconvenience or expense.

All shipments of freight to the buyer's country shall be directed through that country's central freight bureau, and the seller is obliged to make proper contacts and arrangements in all CIF and C&F contracts.

14. Guarantees and Warranties

The seller must deliver goods that are in conformity with the contract concerning quantity, quality (and) description; that are free from any defects or faults in design, workmanship material and manufacturing; and that are packaged in the manner required by the contract and/or these general terms and conditions.

The goods are in conformity with the contract when they are also suitable for the purposes for which goods of the same description would ordinarily be used: are suitable for any particular purpose expressly or implicitly agreed between the parties; possess the qualities of goods that the seller has given to the buyer as a sample or model; and are packaged in the manner usual for such goods or in a manner adequate to preserve and protect the good.

The seller is liable in accordance with the contract and these general terms and conditions for any lack of conformity of the goods with the terms of the contract that exists at the time of the passing of the risk, even though the lack of conformity becomes apparent only after that time.

Unless otherwise provided in the contract, the seller is also liable for any lack of conformity after the time of the acceptance, for a period of 12 (twelve) months thereafter, for breach of any of his obligations under his guarantees or warranties, according to which the goods should remain fit for their intended purpose or should retain specified qualities or characteristics.

15. Remedies

If the seller falls to perform any of his obligations under the contract of these general terms and conditions, the buyer may claim damages and/or exercise other rights as provided in the articles of these general terms and conditions.

At the buyer's option, the seller may, even after the delivery date, remedy at his own expense any failure to perform his obligations if he can do so under conditions acceptable to the buyer.

The buyer may always declare the contract as repudiated if the nonperformance of any of the seller's obligations under the contract is so fundamental that it causes the buyer serious consequences, depriving him of what he was under the circumstances entitled to expect.

The buyer is not deprived of any right he may have to claim damages by exercising his right to other remedies.

16. Exemptions

A party is not liable for failure to perform any of his obligations if he proves that the failure was due to an impediment beyond his control and that he could not have reasonably been expected to take the impediment into account at the time of the conclusion of the contract or to have avoided or overcome it or its consequences, such as fire, mobilization, requisition, embargo, currency and payment restrictions resulting from acts of government, regulations of the central bank, insurrection, war, etc.

The exemption provided by this article has effect only for period during which the impediment exists.

The party who falls to perform must give notice to the other party of the impediment and its effect on his ability to perform. Failure to give notice within a reasonable time after the occurrence of the impediment shall make that party liable for damages resulting from such nonreceipt.

Nothing in this article prevents either party from exercising any right under these general terms and conditions except to claim damages.

17. Third-party Claims

The seller must deliver goods that are free from any right or claim of a third party, either based on industrial property or other intellectual property, or otherwise, unless the buyer has been made aware in writing of the existence of such rights before the conclusion of the purchase contract.

The seller shall hold the buyer exempt from any liability and shall indemnify him for all expenses, costs and damages arising from third-party claim(s), provided the buyer informs him of such claim(s) within a reasonable time after he has become aware of their existence.

18. Settlement of Disputes and Applicable Law

Any dispute, controversy or claim arising out of relating to this contract, or the breach, termination or invalidy thereof, shall be settled by arbitration in accordance with the UN Commission on International Trade Law (UNCITRAL) arbitration rules as at present in force. The number of arbitrators shall be three, and the place of arbitration shall be in the capital of the buyer's country. The language of the arbitration shall be English, and the applicable law shall be the law of the buyer's country. The appointing authority shall be the President of the Permanent Court of Arbitration in the Hague.

7

MONITORING COMPETITORS' PROMOTIONAL ACTIVITIES

PETER SIEBER AND MICHAEL CLEMENTS*

Monitoring competitors' promotional activities in target foreign markets can provide an exporter with highly useful trade information at relatively low cost. The data obtained through such monitoring can serve as a basis for key export marketing decisions including whether to enter a potential target market; what type of marketing strategy is needed for market entry; how to increase the market share when a foothold has already been established; which distribution channels to use; and how much funding to allot to the promotional campaign abroad.

The technique of monitoring promotional activities of competing firms is a marketing tool that has not been widely used in the past but has received more attention in the last year or two. It has the advantage that many aspects of the operation can be carried out in-house with existing marketing staff and at minimal cost. (Specialized commercial firms also exist that

*Peter Sieber and Dr. Michael Clements are the principal executives of Advertising Monitor Ltd., a consultancy firm in the United Kingdom specializing in competitor media analysis.

can undertake such services for a fee.) In addition the results obtained from such monitoring can be obtained in a short time, thereby allowing the export firm's management to take marketing decisions rapidly.

This type of market information exercise could be of particular interest to export managers of small and medium-size firms in developing countries who wish to explore new sales opportunities abroad but lack the funds to visit the markets personally. Some of the techniques described below should be possible to organize within their own marketing departments. Monitoring competitors promotional operations in target foreign markets can provide an exporter with useful trade information at relatively low cost.

What Monitoring is?

This type of market monitoring consists basically of studying the ways in which companies in a specific product line (*i e.* the exporter's competitors) promote their goods in a particular foreign market. By analyzing the form and content of such promotional activities—whether these activities consist of advertising, printed product brochures, store promotions or other means—certain basic facts can be ascertained about these firms market position and their marketing strategies.

For instance, deductions can be made about their market shares, their marketing plans and how these may be changing, the distribution methods they use, the amount of funds they spend on promotional activities, the approximate level of their sales and new developments in their product lines. Such information is important background for an exporter attempting to penetrate the market. The diagram on page 144 shows the role that monitoring can play in the decision making process on market entry.

Monitoring can also often give the company's management its first signal of important new developments in the activities of its competitors, such as the introduction of new products or product modifications: special sales offers or other incentive deals, or approaches to new markets. Early information on such changes allows the management to respond more quickly to the new situation than would otherwise be possible.

The steps in a typical monitoring programme of this kind can be summarized as follows:

1. Determine the types of media and other promotional measures likely to be employed by competing suppliers for the specific product in the markets concerned, so that these can be monitored.

2. Establish access to the relevant trade and other publications required for monitoring, through libraries, subscriptions or press-cutting services. Often a mixture of these is required.

3. Obtain costs for advertising in the various made from the publishers concerned or from the relevant specialist madia publications when available, in order to be able to calculate advertising expenditure of competitors and other marketing details as part of the monitoring exercise.

4. Maintain a register for each advertiser (competitor) with a sample. If possible, of each advertisement that is found as a result of the monitoring. Details on size, colour and cost of the ads should be provided and keyed to a tearsheet (actual copy) or photocopy of the advertisement.

5. Periodically prepare a summary of the total expenditure on advertising for each competitor being monitored. Further statistical processing of the information obtained can be used, for example, to make a trend analysis of advertising expenditure by product and by journal used, for the market as a whole and for its different suppliers.

6. Prepare periodic management summaries on editorial coverage of the competing firms being surveyed and on all other promotional techniques being monitored.

It is usually useful to prepare a dossier for each likely or actual competitor, containing the information gathered under the steps outlined above.

Promotional Activities to be Monitored

The different types of promotional activity that an exporter will need to monitor depend on the kind of product he is supplying and the techniques that his competitors use to promote such goods. Different types of products naturally require different types of promotion. But all promotional programmes are likely to include at least some if not all of the following techniques:

Advertising in the press (in newspapers and magazines) and also possibly on the radio and on television.

Public relations activities (such as making the product known through editorial coverage in the press).

Printed sales material.

Direct mail.

Exhibitions.

Audiovisual sales aids, such as demonstration videos showing a range of products (cosmetics or furniture, for instance) to householders: short, continuous-loop (automatically repeating) film or videos giving pictures and text at exhibitions; and video "catalogues" for salesmen to show to prospective industrial, business or retail buyers. instead of printed material.

Point-of-sale promotion (for instance special displays in stores).

Seminars and product demonstrations.

The weight that a company gives to these different means of promotion may vary considerably, depending on the type of product it supplies and other factors. With consumer products (goods bought by persons for their own personal

TABLE 7.1

Example: Monitoring Report on Company Advertising of Perfume in Conumer Magazines

January 1985

Name of Magazine	*Advertiser*					
	Company A	*Company B*	*Company C*	*Company D*	*Company E*	*Company F*
Company	1×1/2 (1)			1×W (4)		
Cosmopolitan	1×1/2 (1)			1×W (4)		
Honey			1×W 4 cols (3)		1×W 4 cols (5)	
Options	1×1/2 (1)			1×W (4)		
Over 21				1×W (4)		
Woman		1×W 4 cols (2)			1×1/2 (6)	
Woman's Journal		1×W 4 cols (2)			1×1/2 (6)	
Woman's Own		1×W 4 cols (2)			1×W (7)	
Total cost (£)	3,437	33,420	2,420	7,969	19,910	0

Note: The numbers (1), (2), (3) etc are references to separate ad samples and to the written analyses of those ads. The cost figures are based on standard ad insertion costs. 1×1/2=half-page ad; 1×W=full-page ad; 4 cols=4-colour ad.

Source: Ad-Monitor.

use), often as much as 80 per cent of the promotional budget, excluding the cost of the sales force, is spent on advertising in the press and on television. With mail-order selling (sometimes referred to as direct-response selling), on the other hand, advertising and printed matter often absorb a company's entire promotional budget.

Technical and industrial products—from raw materials and components to finished goods, purchased by companies and institutions—require many different kinds of promotional programmes, depending on the product. Since the sales appeal for such items has to be made to a much smaller audience (because the buyers consist of a small target group of individuals in the organizations using the items), fewer and much less costly promotional techniques will generally do the job. The total promotional expenditure for industrial products is usually more evenly split between press advertising, printed matter, exhibitions and direct mail than for consumer products. Television advertising is unlikely to figure significantly in the marketing of industrial products.

An understanding of these differences of emphasis in promotional programmes is required to set up effective monitoring.

How to Monitor

Properlty structured monitoring of the main types of promotion can tell an exporter a great deal about his likely competitors and the products that they have to offer. Most such information can usually be found in competitors' press advertisements and printed sales literature. These, fortunately, are also the types of promotion to which monitoring can most readly be applied. The monitoring of these different methods is discussed below.

Press advertising: Promotions for consumer products usually include advertising in the national press, where available, as well as in the regional and local press. The monitoring of such press advertising should yield both quantitative and qualitative information. It should indicate how much the different competing suppliers are spending on their product ads and how they are spending it.

The relative importance of the national, regional and purely local press differs from country to country, so the monitoring operations will vary accordingly. The United Kingdom and Japan, for example, have a highly developed national press (including both newspapers and magazines). The United Kingdom also has many regional and purely local newspapers. The national press is less well established in the Federal Republic of Germany, although some publications such as Frankfurter Allgemeine Zeitung and Dusseldorf Handelsblatt cover national affairs to some extent. Because of its vast size, the United States has hardly any national newspapers, apart from one or two with country-wide influence such as The Washington Post. The emphasis there is on rigional newspapers. The United States does, however, have a large number of national magazines.

Many different magazines are important advertising media for consumer products, such as foods, cosmetics, household furnishings and equipment. But if consumer products are handled through retail outlets, they also have to be advertised in the trade press (journals and newspapers read specifically by industrial and institutional buyers and by persons involved in the trade and distribution of such products). A great deal of useful information about competitors' products can be obtained from the appropriate trade press. This, after all, is where the manufacturer addresses his own trade. Many aspects of monitoring can be carried out at minimal cost with existing marketing staff.

Quite often the trade press gives more technical and marketing details, as well as illustrations of products, than the more costly national press does. In the national press emphasis tends to be placed more on product image than on factual information about the item. Some suppliers of industrial products and services use the national press for advertising. Most however, concentrate on trade, technical and specialist publications to advertise their products. There are thousands of these publications in Europe alone. These are thus important targets for the monitoring exercise.

For monitoring of advertising to be effective, it must meet a number of requirements:

1. It should be comprehensive, covering all of the publications likely to be used by the competition.

2. It has to be carried out over a period of time to give a continuing record of advertising activity and to show seasonal variations in the ads placed in the trade concerned. An ideal length of time is a full year. But unless monitoring can be done retrospectively, over the past year (at reasonable cost), a full year is usually too long to wait for the results. The minimum period required will depend on the trade or industry. For example, to monitor travel services in Western Europe, the three-month period from December to March will give a very good idea of the general trends. For many lines of Christmas items, such as toys, monitoring the trade press in the spring, and/or the user press from October to December, will be sufficient for an overall view. For most products sold to other businesses, any three-month period will be satisfactory, except for the summer holiday months in Europe and North America.

(The importance of monitoring advertising activity over a sufficient period of time can be illustrated by an actual case. Monitoring recently carried out for a company in the building materials business showed that one of its competitors, which had previously used mainly in-store promotions and company representatives to expand its sales, suddenly began to make a significant shift in its marketing and advertising strategy by starting an extensive publicity campaign in both the consumer and trade press. The continuous monitoring process was sensitive enough to signal this change and to allow the company sponsoring the monitoring exercise to develop its own marketing strategy to meet the new challenge.

3. The monitoring should be correctly costed, giving the money spent for each advertisement that the competition has placed and summaries of the promotional activity of all the advertisers being monitored (the competing suppliers).

4. The monitoring process should make available the actual advertisements so that the information given in the words and pictures of the ads can be studied. This can give a considerable amount of background about the competitor's product and marketing strategies.

It also makes it easier to study the creative approach of the different competing promotional campaigns, providing clues to the way in which buyers are being motivated to purchase the item. Admittedly, the stimuli in the ads are only what the advertisers, and their advertising agencies, believe to be the right ones to entice sales. However the promotional campaigns sponsored by successful companies are almost always based on research and are tested and improved over time. So an analysis of them should provide the exporter with ideas for his own campaign.

Studying the advertisements from different advertisers in the same product line can also provide information about the different sectors of the market to which they appeal, whether it be the top end of the market, the middle segment or the low-priced mass market. This can help an exporter to determine the most suitable market slot for his own product.

The right selection of publications needs to be monitored if the results are to be use to the managers of the export firm. Newspapers. magazines and trade publications can sometimes be consulted in local libraries, although few libraries contain a large selection of specialized trade publications from other countries. Publications can also be obtained from press-cutting agencies that operate nationally, as well as from some that cover the world. Taking out subscriptions is another, although possibly more costly, way to obtain the publications to be monitored.

To determine how much a competing company spends on advertisements, the cost of each individual ad in each publication that is being used must be calculated. Information on such costs is available in what are known as "rate cards" from magazine and newspaper publishers. Advertising rates are also listed in some periodicals such as BRAD (British Rate and Data)

Television and radio: The general monitoring requirements outlined for the written press above apply equally to the audio-visual media. In countries with highly developed television programming, publications exist that give the overall amount spent by each television advertiser. An example of such a publication in the United Kingdom is Quarterly Digest, issued by Media Expenditure Analysis Ltd. It is difficult, however, to determine how this overall expenditure is broken down in terms of length of commercial and the frequency with which it is run, not to mention details on production costs. Furthermore, it is expensive to get copies of the actual commercials. The creative content of commercials is not usually important in the initial phase of monitoring, when the objective is a determine whether or not to enter a market. Once the decision has been taken to launch the product on the export market concerned, however, efforts can be made to obtain videos of the commercials.

Advertising on commercial radio from national or large stations can be monitored in the same way as ads on television. The many small, local stations that exist (particularly in the United States) are less easily monitored. However they are also usually not as likely to play a significant part in the decision of whether or not to enter the market. If radio monitoring is required later, when the marketing strategy is being determined, ways can be found to undertake it. Monitoring can often give a firm the first signals of new activities by its competitors.

Public relations: Not far behind advertising as a valuable source of information on competitors marketing activity is the editorial coverage given by publications to products and services and to the companies that provide them. Most such editorial mention originates with the journalists employed by the publications to write about various business subjects. Editorial coverage may also result from press releases sent out by the suppliers' own public relations (PR) department or by outside consultants hired by it. Press releases are usually carefully scrutinized by the editorial staff, and those that are of interest may be heavily edited or followed up with more information obtained from the company concerned.

A wider range of publications usually has to be monitored to analyze editorial coverage than to study the competitor's advertising. National or local newspapers, for example, might write about a company that would not necessarily use them for its advertising. The different publications to be monitored are, again, accessible to some extent in libraries, by subscription and by employing cutting agencies.

As with the monitoring of advertising, to be a valuable management tool the scrutiny of editorials must cover a wide spectrum of publications and be sustained over a sufficient period of time. The export firm's management should be provided with a periodic summary and appraisal of the relevant editorial coverage. This type of monitoring should be carried out by skilled personnel.

Printed sales material: It is often by monitoring media advertising and PR coverage that an exporter can find out who the competing suppliers are, so that their sales literature can be studied. There is usually no difficulty in getting such printed publicity material. Either it can be applied for directly or obtained through a third party. This material can be analyzed in a manner similar to that used for advertisements.

Direct mail: It hould also be possible to be included in the appropriate lists of competing suppliers' automatic mailings of publicity and sales material, either in the exporter's own name or that of a third person. The same type of monitoring used for other printed matter can be carried out for this material.

Exhibition catalogues: Nothing can replace a personal visit to an exhibition as a means of seeing what products competing companies are promoting and how they are promoting them. However this is often prohibitively expensive for small exporters in developing countries. The exhibition catalogue alone usually gives a great deal of useful information and can be carefully analyzed as part of the general monitoring operation. It tells not only who is exhibiting but also indirectly indicates how much each exhibitor is spending on his exhibition site, from the position and size of his stand. In many cases the catalogue also gives valuable details on product ranges featured by the exhibitors. Catalogues are available from exhibition organizers and are often worth their weight in gold for an assessment of the competition.

Audiovisual sales aids, point-of-sale activities, seminars and other promotional efforts are less easily monitored from outside the country than the techniques reviewed above. They are also, however, far less important for an exporter to follow and analyze in the initial phase of market entry.

Monitoring for Established Brands

The opportunities and procedures for monitoring brands that are already established in the market are much the same as those described above for unbranded products. The benefits are also very similar, although with some subtle differences. In the case of branded items, much is usually already known and published about the rival products and companies, their shares of the market and their strategies, so monitoring does not provide much new information in this sense. What it can give is a constant, on-going picture of these elements. In this situation the monitoring can be carried out more readily and relatively more economically than for nonbranded goods. It can give the management of the export firm a regular check on the competitors' activities.

The optimum reporting period for branded items depends on the market. Monthly reporting is the norm. In rapidly moving markets, however, weekly reporting is required.

Example

To illustrate the monitoring operations described above, assume that Exporter X in a developing country wishes to enter one of three possible European markets with his range of small wooden toys. Because he does not have a sufficiently large budget to visit the markets in person, he decides to ask his marketing manager to monitor the promotional activities of other firms supplying toys in the markets of the United Kingdom, France and the Federal Republic of Germany, and to obtain key marketing data on them so that he can make a decision on market entry.

The marketing manager therefore draws up a plan of action for the monitoring operation, which consists of analyzing the following:

1. Press advertising: Obtain access to the following magazines and newspapers to be monitored in the United Kingdom:

Trade press: British Toys and Hobbies, Toy Trader, Toys International and the Retailer, and Toys 'N' Playthings.

Each of these publications is to be scanned for three months (January to March). It may be necessary (depending on the starting date of the project) to conduct a retrospective study of these publications.

Consumer press (here the choice of publication will depend upon the type of toy and its price range):

If it is a popular, low-priced toy, then monitor: Radio Times, TV Times, Daily, Mirror, Sunday Mirror and News of the World.

It the item is more up-market, higher in price, monitor: Radio Times, TV Times, Sunday Times, The Observer, The Daily Telegraph and Sunday Telegraph.

Each of these publications is to be scanned from the beginning of October to the end of December.

Check for possible mail-order (direct-response) campaigns, that is, companies offering to supply direct against payment or on a charge basis, using a credit card.

Check also the toy sections in major mail order catalogues. (For instance John Moores Group and Great Universal Stores Group publish glossy catalogues that are supplied, on request, direct to households.)

A similar review of relevant publications is to be conducted for France and the Federal Republic of Germany.

Publications are to be scanned for three months for advertising of suppliers of wooden toys, and a summary of the results is to be presented to the company's manager every four weeks.

A final report is to be prepared at the end of the period giving the following information on each company, as well as copies of the actual ads monitored:

Its advertising expenditure.

Its advertising them , and along with this, if possible, its overall marketing strategy.

Details on its product line, and any new development in its products.

The segment of the market to which it is directed.
Its distribution channels.

This information will be used by the management to make the following marketing decisions: It will indicate the spread and intensity of competitor ad activity which publications are dominated by which toy manufacturers and which are not; and it will indicate the scale of expenditure necessary to make the same kind of impact in the market place.

2. Press editorial coverage: Obtain access to the following magazines and newspapers to be monitored in the United Kingdom, in addition to those mentioned under (1.) above. Daily Mail, Daily Express, Star, Mail on Sunday, Sunday People, Lady, Mother and Parents.

Each of these publications is to be monitored from the beginning of October to the end of December. The trade papers listed in (1.) above should be monitored from January to March at least, and for the whole year if possible.

Interim summaries are required every four weeks.

A similar monitoring of relevant publications should be conducted for France and the Federal Republic of Germany.

The information to be sought through such scanning:

New developments in the marketing strategies of competitors.

Any changes in competitors' product lines.

Any indications of market share and total sales in the market.

The information obtained will be used to assess the impact made by competitors in these publications (other than that achieved by classified ads). It can also indicate further competitor maketing strategy (for new products, for instance) including future advertising activity.

3. Printed sales material: Write to a selected list of companies in each of the three countries; request copies of these firms' most recent sales literature for wooden toys. The information to be obtained through this exercise consists of the same type of details sought above in press advertising.

The management can use this information to determine the scope of the monitoring exercise—through identification of the main competitors—as well as details on product ranges, prices and (often) distributor outlets.

4. Direct mail: Write to the same companies as those under (3.) above, asking to be put on their automatic mailing list to receive all company promotional and other literature. The information expected to be obtained:

The same details as under (1.) and (3.) above.

The decisions affected by this information are identical to those under (1.) above, particularly the level of effect put into direct mail, as opposed to press advertising.

5. Exhibition catalogues: Write to the organizers of trade fairs in the three countries for their latest catalogues, for instance of the Harrogate International Toy Fair in the United Kingdom.

The information to be deducated from this material:

Expenditure of competitors on fair participation.

Product ranges of competing firms.

Trade prices and discounts, and margins

New product developments.

These details will be helpful in taking decisions on whether it is necessary to consider attendance at trade fairs as part of the total promotional activity.

Management must decide on the basis of the data collected whether to proceed further with the project. In practice, clients decide to continue the monitoring activity after launching the product to note subsequent changes in competitor marketing and advertising activity caused by their market entry.

Monitoring Services Available

With a dedicated and skilled staff, much of the monitoring described in this article can be undertaken in-house by an export company, with only library facilities and press-cutting services required from the outside.

In addition, however, there are firms that specialize in providing monitoring services on a commercial basis. Generally speaking, such commercial services are well advanced in the Scandinavian countries, the United Kingdom and, for certain geographical regions. in the United States. Since the type and range of monitoring services vary not only from one country to the next but also between different industries and trades, and are rapidly changing, it is not possible to provide a comprehensive review here of the services available throughout the world. The list below indicates some of the principal services that exist in the United Kingdom and also several international services available from that country.

When commercial monitoring services are required in other countries, information on them can usually be obtained from an appropriate trade organization in the country concerned, the local member of the International Association of Advertising Agencies, or the national associations of publishers and of television and radio networks. Commercial officers in embassies can also often furnish details on possible monitoring services in their home country.

Examples of international monitoring services:

1. Ad-Monitor: Advertising Monitor Ltd. offers tailor-made monitoring services of press advertising and editorial coverage

anywhere in the world. concerning publications of all kinds. The agency can provide reports on advertising costs and on current and past advertising expenditure by companies; press cuttings of editorials on specific companies; and special monitoring of sales promotion of all kinds anywhere in the world. (Address: 2 North Grove, London N6.) (See also the discussion below.)

2. Adtrack: Offers European-wide coverage of advertising consisting of monthly monitoring reports on advertisements in 5 major produced groups (in the automotive, business equipment, travel, home electronics and photographic categories) in 12 countries. (Address: Landsear House, London WC2H.)

3. Micro-Monitor: Issues special reports on the advertising appearing in micro-computer publications in the United Kingdom, France and the Federal Republic of Germany. (Address: Lange Annastraat 30, 2011 XJ Haarlem, Netherlands)

4. Romeike and Curtice: Probably the oldest press-cutting service in Europe, if not the world. It provides press cuttings of advertisements and editorial coverage on any industry group or on selected organizations or companies. (It is therefore one of the sources of in-house monitoring.) Using a network of other press-cutting services, it offers an international service covering media throughout the world. (Address: Hale House. 290-296 Green Lanes, London N10.)

Examples of monitoring services covering only the U.K. market:

1. MEAL (Media Expenditure Analysis Ltd.): Publishes Quarterly Digest, widely used in the United Kingdom, which gives total brand expenditure with a standard data base of competitor advertising expenditure covering television, the national press, provincial Sunday newspapers. general publication titles, women's magazines, and some technical and trade

publications in the country. The agency also produces reports on selected product groups, as well as reports on eight specialist subjects including agriculture, computers and commercial vehicles. Details are available by brand as well as by cost, the firms's information is available on computer (printout, tapes and on-line) and on microfiche. (Address: 63 St. Martin's Lane, London WC2.)

2. Media Monitoring Services: Offers a range of reports on advertising in the medical and prescription pharmaceutical markets. It has five standard services grouped under such headings as analysis by product, journal or medical grouping, (Address: 9 Crossways Sunninghill, Ascot, Berks BL5 OPY, United Kingdom.)

3. BRAD (British Rate and Data): Gives the advertising rates for virtually all U.K. publications, as well as the principal advertising rates for commercial television and radio in the United Kingdom. (Address: Sovereign Way, Tonbridge, Kent TN9 IRW, United Kingdom.)

How an agency works: As an example of how an agency works, Ad-Monitor (listed above) will monitor press advertising and editorial coverage in the countries that the client specifies and on the companies (the advertisers) or products that the client indicates. The agency's reports to clients on advertising give an analysis of the cost of each ad monitored, together with the actual tearsheet of the advertisement (the printed page of the published ad). A breakdown of what the advertisers have spent in the past (usually during the last year), as well as reports on their on-going expenditure (usually monthly, but weekly when required), can also be obtained. Press cuttings of editorials are accompanied by periodic qualitative appraisals of the discussion of the firms in these texts. The agency also executes special programmes to monitor sales promotion of other kinds when a client so requests.

Published fees apply to some of the agency's standard services, but most of its assignments must be costed individually. Estimates for a particular job are available free of charge.

Costs of using an agency: Costs for a monitoring assignment depend on a number of different factors—the number of advertisers to be monitored, the number of publications to be studied, the number of countries and time available for the project. For many clients it is preferable to break the project down into a number of parts and provide detailed costings on each segment. This avoids the global estimate that might put off the potential user and it also allows the client to draw up a list of priorities for researching. For example, the client might decide to monitor the United Kingdom first (on the basis of prior market research), then France and so on.

For the wooden toy example in the United Kingdom discussed above, for instance, Ad-Monitor would charge from £500 to £1,000 for the three months (this includes both advertising and press editorial coverage). How costs are built up:

Covering five advertisers in the trade press only, from £600 per year; monthly reports provided.

Covering five advertisers in the trade and technical press with press cuttings, from £1,000 per year, plus a small charge for cuttings; monthly reports issued.

Covering five advertisers in newspapers and the consumer, trade and technical press, with press cuttings, from £2,000 a year plus the cuttings charges; monthly reports.

Usually the monitoring of five major competitors is sufficient to provide the client with a clear. concise view of the competitive situation. There are occasions, however, when it is desirable to extend the coverage beyond five advertisers. The scale of charges for a wider coverage does not increase in the same proportion as the increase in numbers covered.

Retrospective reviews for the United Kingdom start at £2,000 and are more costly if the exercise entails a wide scope of interest.

Other countries can be monitored from the United Kingdom or "on site." Specific prices have to be quoted for each job. Other operations also have to be quoted individually (for instance for statistical forecasting).

In the example of the wooden toy company, the minimum cost, for five advertisers, would be in the range of £2,000 to £4,000 for the three countries mentioned.

8

IMPORT OPERATIONS

I

FINDING THE RIGHT SUPPLIER*

One of the keys to successful importing is locating the most suitable source of supply. Success in procurement operations depends to a large extent on the efforts made at the beginning of the purchasing cycle to identify appropriate suppliers. If the supplier who is selected turns out to be unsuitable and fails to fulfill his contractual obligations, the legal steps that can be taken against him are of only limited practical use. What a purchasing department is interested in is receiving its supplies at the right time and according to specifications. The basic mechanism for achieving the desired results is therefore the proper selection of suppliers.

The Selection Process

The process of selecting suppliers in international procurement consists of five basic steps:

*By B. Bhattacharyya, associate professor at the Indian Institute of Foreign Trade, New Delhi.

1. Determine the requirements of what is to be purchased.
2. Identify suitable potentiil suppliers.
3. Assess the reliability and capability of those sources.
4. Register the potential suppliers.
5. Review suppliers' performance periodically.

The principal elements involved in each of those steps are outlined below.

Determining Requirements

The import needs of the business firm or government department must be clearly specified. Details must be provided on what type of product is required, stated in technical terms rather than trade jargon. The deadlines for receiving the required goods must also be precisely determined. It is only when this step has been taken that the process of locating a supplier can be started.

Identifying Potential Suppliers

The next step is to draw up a list of suitable sources from which the goods in question can be purchased. This is an important task, because only when there are a sufficient number of qualified potential suppliers, resulting in a competitive market situation, can the best terms of purchase be obtained. Even the opening of a global tender does not in itself guarantee that a large number of suppliers will be available from which to choose—if the size of the contract is small, large suppliers may not be interested in bidding on it, or some of the potential suppliers may not even see the published tender notice.

Therefore, a buyer needs to identify a sufficiently long list of suitable potential suppliers. Inhouse sources can be used for this, as well as other types of information. The sources are basically the following:

1. If the organization has purchased the item in question in the past, through tenders or by some other method,

information should be readily available in the purchasing department on the performance of those previous suppliers.

2. Many countries, including some developing countries, publish exporter directories, generally on an annual basis. Directories of this type contain a list of exporters classified by product and also sometimes gives details such as the company's paid-up capital and the name of its banker. International directories and specialized publications (such as the Kompass series, published by Kompass Publishers, Windsor Court, East Grinstead House, Fast Grinstead, West Sussex RH19 IXD, U.K.) are other useful sources for identifying potential suppliers.
3. When complex items are imported, it may be necessary to invite applications from prospective suppliers or manufacturers through advertisements that indicate the requirements of the goods to be purchased.

Reliability and Capability

When the potential suppliers have been identified, the next question is how to select those that are most reliable and the most suitable to furnish the goods. These factors can be assessed by looking at the:

1. Quality of the product they supply.
2. Regularity of their supplies of that product.
3. Price of the product.
4. Supply capacity in relation to the buyer's needs.
5. After-sales service (where required) for the item.
6. Financial soundness of the company.

An evaluation can be made of the supplier at various stages in the procurement process. Two of the most important stages for such an assessment are:

Fig. 8-A Supplier Evaluation Scheme: Factors to Consider

Production	*Price*	*Performance*
1. Capacity	1. Price level	1. Portion of orders accepted out of total orders placed
2. Qualification and experience of staff employed	2. Price maintenance	2. Lead time required
3. In-process quality control	3. Discount structure	3. Adherence to quality standards
4. Cost control procedures	4. Credit terms	4. Adherence to delivery schedule
5. Preventive maintenance	5. Price for spare parts	5. Acceptance of small-value orders
6. Research and development facilities	6. Cost of other ofter-sales service	6. Acceptance of orders of custom-made items
7. Manufacturing history	7. Shipment terms	7. Replacement of defective items
		8. Discrepancies in documents
		9. Record of after-sales service
		10. Record of settlement of disputes

1. When potential suppliers are being identified.
2. After the suppliers has been selected and has started making shipments, for example, six to twelve months after his first consignment has arrived.

At the initial stage, the objective is to analyze whether a prospective supplier is qualified or not, before the order is placed. The post-shipment evaluation is used to assess the past performance of the supplier in order to decide whether he should be retained as a source in the future. The information on which the initial evaluation is made is limited to such details as production data, bank references, third-party recommendations and the commercial reputation of the supplier. At the post-shipment stage of evaluation, many more elements should be available for the assessment, including the degree to which the supplier fulfilled his contractual obligations.

It is desirable to develop a specific evaluation procedure for suppliers. This will help ensure that the assessments made of the different sources of supply are consistent and that all of the relevant factors are given due consideration each time.

A general scheme for a supplier evaluation is shown in the box above. For the evaluation at the initial stage, the elements shown under the heading "Production" should be considered, while for the post-shipment evaluation, the factors under all three headings should be taken into account.

The next step is to develop a questionnaire to collect information on these elements. The questionnaire must be precise and should ask for information that will indicate the supplier's capability and reliability.

Prospectitive suppliers should not be requested to provide a mass of information that has no relevance for the matter at hand, as this may dampen their enthusiasm for supplying the goods. The purchasing department should be selective in seeking information.

The type of information needed will vary, depending on the category of supplier. For example, information required on a broker operating in a commodity exchange will have little in common with that needed on a manufacturer. A standard questionnair can, however, be prepared, irrespective of the classification of the supplier. A note can be added in the appropriate columns in the questionnaire to indicate that the supplier can leave certain columns blank if he is, for example, a manufacturer or a trader.

An example of a simple questionnaire is given on pages 155 to 157. For most items purchased, this form should suffice. Depending on the characteristics of the product being purchased, however, it may be necessary to add other points to the questionnaire.

Registration

Registration, or the listing of approved suppeliers, is the formal method of completing the process of evaluation and of short-listing the prospective suppliers. Only suppliers who rank among the highest on the basis of the evaluation scheme are listed on the register.

The basic advantage of registration is that the buyer can approach the priority supplying firms immediately and ask for offers. The lead time between identifying the import need and placing the order is thus considerably reduced, compared with a situation in which the buyer has to start from scrateh to find probable suppliers or go through the routine procedure of announcing tenders. From the standpoint of the suppliers, the benefit of registration is that they are the only parties who receive the notices for goods to be purchased on the basis of nonadvertised tenders. Some purchasing departments also walve the equirement of submitting a bank guarantee for registered suppliers who submit offers.

APPENDIX

QUESTIONNAIRE FOR SUPPLIER REGISTRATION

Mail to:

General instruction: This questionnaire must be completed in (name of the language). All enclosures must also be in (language). The financial report from the bank should be sent directly.

1. Name:......................

2. Mailing address:......................

   Cable:......................

   Telex: ....

3. Classification of business (check appropriate box):

   *Private firm

   *Public department

   *State enterpise

   *Subsidiary

4. If a subsidiary, name of the parent company:...................

5. Classification of applicant:

   *Manufacturer

   *Sole selling agent

   *Local agent

   *Trade

   *Other (give details)..............................

6. If applicant is sole selling agent or a locala gent, name of the principal:.............................

7. If applicant is not a local agent, is there a local agent?

   ☐ Yes ☐ No

   Is yes, his address:

   Cable: ....

   Telex:...........................

8. If applicant is an agent:

   a. Agency agreement valid until:

   b. Rate of commission is:

Product	Rate
....	....
....	....

   c. Can the commission be paid in local currency?

   ☐ Yes ☐ No

   d. Name and address of the technical facilities available for servicing:..........................

9. Details of products for which registration is being sought:

Product	Specifications	Production capacity	Quantity being offered
....	....	....	....
....	....	....	....

10. Export experience:

Year	Product	Quantity	Importing country
....	....	....	....
....	....	....	....

11. Already registered with:
    Government department (specify):........................
    ....
    State enterprise (specify):..................................

Other (specify).........................

12. Name of banker:.............................. ...
    Address:.......................

---

13. Enclosures (check):

*Capacity report.

*Technical report.

*Catalogues and price lists.

*Standard warranty or guarantee conditions.

*Agency agreement.

*Balance sheet.

*Third-party recommendation.

*Copy of letter asking the bank to send confidential report directly to buyer.

Reviewing Performance

Registration is generally valid for a fixed period, such as from one to three years. When that period expires, the firm has to register again. Some purchasing departments, on the other hand, have an indefinite period of registration, but they review the list periodically. If a supplier's performance is below standard, his name is taken off the list. Whatever the system, there must be a well organized procedure for periodically reviewing the performance of suppliers on the list, such as the evaluation scheme discussed above.

Conclusion

Identifying and selecting suitable suppliers is crucial for effective import management. A Systematic approach can help achieve this objective.

II

ESSENTIAL ELEMENTS OF INTERNATIONAL TENDERING*

Tendering is a fundamental aspect of the public procurement of goods and services. The process of public procurement is started at the initiative of the responsible agency, which solicits offers from potential suppliers of the goods and services in question. In the case of public procurement these offers are often referred to as tenders, thereby denoting the formal character of the offer. In a broader context, offers are also referred to as "bids," "proposals" or "quotations." Tenders

*Gosta Westring. By Senior Procurement Adviser at the World Bank. The article is extracted from International Procurement: A Training Manual, published jontly by the World Bank, the UN Institute for Training and Research (UNITAR) and ITC.

are normally invited on a competitive basis from several interested parties. "Competitive tendering" or "competitive bidding" —often referred to merely as "tendering" or "bidding"— is the standard practice for public procurement. Some systems also envisage the use of "single tendering," thus admitting that just one tender may be invited in certain exceptional cases in which competition may be excluded, inappropriate or unavailable.

The Tendering Process

Tendering is a formal procedure by which competing bids for a particular contract are invited, received and evaluated, whereupon the contract is awarded to the tenderer who has submitted the most advantageous bid.

Tendering can be either "open" or "selective. The procedure is called open when tender are invited through advertisements or other forms of public notice from any eligible party. In the case of selective tenders a limited number of firms are invited by the contracting agency to submit offers. The agency can select the tenderers either through its previous knowledge of the market or after a prequalification procedure, in which eligible firms are invited to provide evidence of their ability to perform the services or produce goods desired by the agency.

The following information is normally requested from firms for prequalification:

(a) Contractor's identification.

(b) Experience and past performance.

(c) Personnel.

(d) Equipment.

(e) Financial status.

(f) Present commitments.

(g) Personnel and equipment available for the proposed contract.

(h) Broad plan of the execution of works.

To ensure uniformity of presentation, prequalification documents usually contain a set of questionnaires covering the main areas of information required.

Key Features of Tendering

Among the essential elements of standard international procurement procedures are those adopted in relation to the World Bank Guidelines for Procurement and the GATT Agreement on Government Procurement. The following section reviews the essential elements of tendering (or "competitive bidding)", based on the World Bank guidelines, the GATT agreement and national government practice.

The key features of tendering can be summarized under ten headings:

1. Suitable package.
2. Early warning.
3. Non-discrimination.
4. Accessibility.
5. Neutrality.
6. Formality.
7. Confidentiality.
8. Consistency
9. Objectivity.
10. No negotiation before award.

Suitable Package

Procurement planning, whether it be for a specific project or for recurrent inputs to operate a plant or facility, should, aim to attract maximum competition from large and small, and domestic and foreign, tenderers. Increasing the size and complexity of contracts may reduce the scope for competition, particularly by domestic suppliers. Large contracts, on the other hand, attract the attention of potential bidders on the international market. Thus, devising a suitable package amounts to a balancing act with many factors to be borne in mind. One generally accepted manner of easing this balancing act is to allow partial bids under alternative contract options so as to attract the interest of both small and large firms.

Early Warning

Competitive tendering can be organized on either an open or a selective basis. Most international lending agencies and governments have an information service that helps disseminate news about major projects to be undertaken in the future. The international agencies use for this purpose a United Nations periodical. Development Business (formerly Development Forum, Business Edition). In which a description is given of new projects and the scope of good and services to be procured in connection with them. The GATT agreement envisages a similar announcement procedure, which will give interested firms an opportunity to prepare themselves for participation in the subsequent round of bidding.

Next, tenders are invited with an adequate number of days in which to prepare bids. According to the international lending agencies, the interval between invitation and submission of bids should be not less than 90 days in any case of international bidding and not less than 90 days for large civil works contracts. The GATT agreement, which refers only to product and not to works, stipulates a minimum period of 30 days, while stressing that "any prescribed timelimit shall be adequate to allow foreign as well as domestic suppliers to prepare and submit tenders before the closing of the tendering procedures."

The "early warning system" must also contain safeguards to assure that the tendering invitation actually comes to the knowladge of those concerned. For selective tendering this would be less of a problem, since invitations to tender are sent directly to those selected. In that case, the emphasis on widespread publicity is at an earlier stage, when news about the investment decision is distributed. Interested firms should at this stage get a chance to apply for inclusion on the list of selected tenderers.

Open tender notices and invitations to prequalify, on the other hand, must be based on advertisements and notices to official commercial representatives. Advertisements should be made in official gazettes or widely circulated newspapers, and for major contracts also in specialized magazines. Publication of such invitations in Development Business is also required by the international financing institutions.

Non-discrimination

This is one aspect of policy on which national and international agencies tend to diverge. Government contracts in industrialized countries are let to an increasing extent on the basis of selective rather than open tendering, or through negotiation with one or more selected firms. The European Development Fund (EDF) rules (of the European Community) outlined in the EDF Draft General Conditions for Works do not express a preference for open tendering over selective tendering. The GATT agreement does not express a preference for one or the other method, either. It stipulates that selection of tenderers shall be done in a "fair and non-discriminatory manner. The agreement calls upon responsible agencies, in order to "ensure optimum effective international competition under selective tendering procedures" to "invite tenders from the maximum number of domestic and foreign suppliers, consistent with the efficient operation of the procurement." The World Bank normally requires its borrowers to obtain goods and works through international competitive bidding open to all eligible bidders. The Bank's guidelines do not refer to selective tendering as a suitable method for international competitive bidding, but do admit that pre-qualification can be advisable for large or complex contracts in order to ensure, in advance of bidding that invitations are confined to capable firms. The pre-qualification procedure is based on advertisements and notifications of the same kind as those that are used for open tendering and all interested firms may present their "credentials" to prove that they command the necessary experience, capabilities and financial resources.

This may be one aspect of the Bank's guidelines in which the Bank's international status calls for a different policy from that which is favoured by national government. The interest of the borrowing government in "filtering" potential bidders in order to make the scrutiny and evaluation of bids more manageable has to be balanced against the interest of other member governments in securing maximum bidding opportunities for their own exporters. Procurement entities must be available to answer questions about the proposed contract.

Accessibility

In order to allow for realistic competition, tenderers must be given adequate time in which to prepare their bids. The time normally stipulated was referred to above on the need for an early warning.

Procurement entities must also facilitate the work of the tenderers in other ways. They must marke themselves available, while tenders are being prepared, to answer questions about the proposed contract. They must provide the bidding documents to interested firms in an expedient manner and at a reasonable cost. That cost should be related to the cost of document reproduction only, not to the cost of preparing specification and other relevant material.

Accessibility is also affected by the use of socalled tender guarantees or bid bonds. This type of instrument is defined by Uniform Rules for Contract Guarantees of the international Chamber of Commerce as: "an undertaking given by a bank, insurance company or other party ("the guarantor") at the request of a tenderer ("the principal") or given on the instructions of a bank, insurance company, or other party so requested by the principal ("instructing party") to a party inviting tenders ("the beneficiary") whereby the guarantor undertakes—in the event of default by the principal in the obligations resulting from the submission of the tender—to make payment to the beneficiary within the limits of a stated sum of money."

The purpose of the bid bond is to provide an assurance that the tenderer is prepared to sign the contract if his tender is accepted. The World Bank guidelines admit that bid security may be required in order to afford the procurement entity reasonable protection, but the guidelines do not specify the instances in which this type of security is needed. It is often used in connection with major contracts as a precaution to ward off unrealistic bids. Bid bonds should not, however, be set so high as to discourage suitable bidders from tendering. The EDF Draft General Conditions for Works limit the amount of any tender guarantee to one per cent of the contract value. Under national systems, guarantees are sometimes required for a higher amount.

The fact that tender validity periods tend to be stretched out over periods of many months—and are often prolonged—adds to the risk that tender guarantees can become quite a heavy burden on the tenderers. They definitely limit access to competition, and should be used in appropriate instances only. A relevant criterion would be to measure the value of the contract against the financial turnover of the potential tenderers. In the case of vehicles, for instance, manufacturers turnover figures are vastly superior to the value of any individual order. In such cases, there is no need for a tender guarantee, since no tenderer is likely to go back on his offer due to financial difficulties intervening during the tendering period. Works contracts, on the other hand, may represent a very large proportion of one contractor's turnover, which increases the risk that he might have second thoughts after placing his tender, depending on other events affecting his business. In such situation it may be a good idea to insist on tender guarantees.

The GATT code mention "financial guarantees" (Article V:4 (f) and V:12(f), but contatns no rules or guidelines as to their amounts. Governments of European countries do not use them frequently.

Neutrality

In the case of specifications, the bidding documents. In the language of the World Bank guidelines, should be worded so as to encourage international competitive bidding. To that end, no particular national standard should be preferred in specifications of the goods and services to be procured.

Specifications for equipment should be based on performance requirements rather then on design and should avoid reference to a particular trademark or brand name. If such reference is necessary in order to describe the goods to be procured, the words "or equivalent" must be added in order to permit acceptance of offers for similar products. The World Bank rules in this regard conform to normal government practice and to the GATT agreement.

General conditions of the contract to be awarded constitute an important part of the bidding documents. Procurement entities may obtain a more favourable market response if they invite tenders on the basis of neutral general conditions, *i.e.*, conditions that are worked out by some third party without favouring any particular party to the contract. The World Bank guidelines contain some reminders about clauses that ought to be inserted in general conditions. In addition to price and payment clauses, but theses provisions are of an indicative nature and leave it to the drafter of each set of bidding documents to choose general conditions suited to the circumstances at hand.

The Bank does not recommend any particular set of general conditions for the various types of contracts it finances. It does exert some influence on the drafting of bidding documents, partly by reserving for itself the right, according to individual loan agreements, to check the bidding documents for any particular contract, and partly by making available for the guidance of borrowers sample bidding documents for goods and works. (Sample bidding documents can be obtained from the Asian Development Bank, Inter-American Development Bank, the World Bank and other international development finance institutions).

Formality

Tendering is a formal process that involves set procedures for the submission and opening of bids. This implies that:

Tenders must be submitted in written form. Tenders submitted by telex, telegram or telecopy must be confirmed by mall.

Tenders should normally be submitted in scaled envelopes. Tenders must be delivered to a certain place before a certain time specified in the invitation to tender. Late tenders should be returned unopened unless the delay is caused by by circumstances beyond the tenderer's control, and the acceptance of the late tender does not give the bidder any undue advantage.

Tenders should be opened at the time stipulated for delivery or promptly thereafter. The international lending institutions, and many governments, prefer that bid opening take place in public. Other governments permit opening in a private, recorded session. The GATT agreement requires procurement entitles to open tenders in the presence of either tenderers or their representatives or an appropriate and impartial witness. The procedure for opening of tenders seems to be one formal aspect on which a measure of disagreement exists. Some governments and entities feel that opening, including the announcement of prices quoted by the tenderers, in a recorded, private session, subject to the control of the auditing arm of government, is sufficient. Others—including international finance institutions such as the World Bank and the regional development banks—have come to consider that the public opening is an additional, necessary safeguard against manipulations of the tendering contest. It also helps assure tenderers that their bid has been received and will be considered.

If in response to a query about the bidding documents from one firm, the procurement entity wants to clarify any part of the bidding documents. It should communicate the same information to all propective tenderers.

Confidentiality

Prior to bid opening, envelopes containing tenders must be checked to see that they are property sealed. They must be kept in a safe place until opened and recorded. No copies should be taken of the documents, and other suitable measures should be envisaged to ensure that their contents are not divulged to persons other than those officially responsible for their examination. Those persons must be properly instructed in the handling of tenders and should be under an obligation to observe strict confidentiality. Internal controls should be organized with a view to discovering, at an early stage, any malpractices.

Consistency

When tenders have been received and recorded, they should be checked for possible errors, correct signatures and adherence to stipulated requirements in the bidding documents. If a bid is not "substantially responsive" to the bidding documents; or contains inadmissible reservations, it should not be considered. This important stipulation in the World Bank guidelines is paralleled by the GATT agreement, according to which" a tender must, at the time of opening, conform to the essential requirements of the notices or tender documentation and be from suppliers which comply with the conditions for participation. "To procurement entities, it may seem tempting at times to accept non-responsive tenders. The World Bank and GATT rules give some leeway in this direction, too, by referring to "substantially" responsive and "essential" requirements. This means that the procurement entity can accept minor deviations from the tender documents, while in return attaching some form of penality to the deviation in the subsequent evaluation.

Those tenders that, upon examination, have qualified as "substantially" responsive must be given serious consideration. Although many agencies reserve for themselves in the invitation to tender the right to reject any and all bids without having to provide any justification or remedy, they should, as a matter of good public administration and business policy:

(a) Have all necessary authorizations and financial resources to go ahead with the contract following an invitation to tender.

(b) Give consideration to all eligible tenders received.

(c) Award the contract to the tenderer who has submitted the most advantageous bid in terms of price and any other evalution criteria spelled out in the bidding documents.

Objectivity

The purpose of evaluation is to determine the lowest evaluated bid. The lowest bid is not necessarily the most advantageous one, considering all relevant factors. Price is obviously the first—but rarely the only—criterion that has to be born in mind. The procurement entity therefore has to decide what factors in addition to price it is going to consider and to describe them to prospective tenderers in clear terms. In the absence of objective criteria, the award of the contract becomes an arbitrary matter. Tenderers, like competitors in any sport are not likely to enter into competition without knowing the rules of the game. Thus, objective evaluation criteria have to be formulated, spelled out in the bidding documents and applied in a consistent manner. Preferably, the criteria should be capable of being expressed in monetary terms. Examples of cases where it is possible to adjust the bid price in relation to other evaluation criteria are late or early delivery, capacity (for instance the tractive power of a locomotive or the steam generating capacity of a boiler), and cost of operation and maintenance. Other evaluation criteria are necessarily of a more subjective nature, such as the maneuverability and reliability of equipment.

The examples quoted in the foregoing paragraph demonstrate that it is more easily said than done to formulate and apply objective evaluation criteria.

No Negotiation before Award

The logical conclusion of the tender competition is to select a winner on the basis of the stated criteria without any effort at obtaining a better price or some other fovour from any tenderer. The World Bank guidelines are very clear on this point: No bidder shall be asked or permitted to change the substance or price of his bid. The European Development Fund and other regional financing institutions follow the same principle. So do many governments.

Other governments reserve for themselves the right to negotiate with tenderers. The GATT agreement foresees the possibility of negotiation and stipulates: "if it appears from evaluation that no one tender is obviously the most advantageous . . .the entity shall in any subsequent negotiations (underlining added here), give equal consideration and treatment to all tenders within the competitive range."

The GATT agreement seems to leave a substantial measure of freedom to negotiate with tenderers, provided the responsible entities limit tendering to those firms that have submitted tenders within "the competitive range" and deal in a non-discriminatory way with those firms.

One important commercial aspect must be borne in mind when deciding whether or not to allow negotiation in connection with competitive tendering: Tenders are likely to be for one amount it tenderers know that contract award will follow without any previous negotiation, and for a different amount if they expect to be called for negotiations before award. Their tenders may include a margin for reduction in the bargaining phase. Another possibility is that their bids will be unrealistically low, based on the hope that they will be able to compensate themselves in more or less obvious ways in the course of negotiations. Thus the option to negotiate may jeopardize the main purpose of the tender competition, namely to extract the lowest responsive and responsible—offer from each tenderer.

Competitive Negotiation

It is indeed a most interesting and difficult, task to define in what instances competitive tendering principles should be discarded in favour of negotiated procurement and to define for these cases an appropriate procedure designed to maintain fair competition, objectivity and non-discrimination. These would be instances, then, of a different kind from the ordinary cases of direct purchase, involving, for example spare parts, repeat orders and proprietary articles, where no scope for competition exists. The case in point is the complex project that cannot conveniently be divided into separate contracts for design, supply, erection construction and supervision. The need for coordination between the various project elements may be so strong as to favour a contract of the turnkey type that integrates all or most of these project inputs. To what extent are the ten points listed above relevant to procurement on a negotiated basis between firms competing for this type of contract ?

Early warning signals can certainly be sent out to interested companies in order to allow time for preparation of offers. Negotiated procurement can be carried out in a non-discriminatory way in the same manner as competitive tendering can be limited to firms selected from registers or from a pre-qualification exercise. Competition for negotiated contracts can be made accessible by measures designed to facilitate competing firms' participation in the process of procurement. The one important reservation in this regard concerns tender bonds. While it is quite acceptable to apply this sort of assurance in some cases of competitive tendering in order to ward off unrealistic bids, the situation is different in negotiated procurement. It is obviously unfair to negotiate with a bidder under the threat of calling his tender bond.

The problem of drafting clear and neutral specification is a very real one. This problem is not unique to negotiated procurement, however. International competitive bidding is often based on performance specifications that will render it necessary to compare products and services which, although serving the same purpose, bear separate technical characteristics. Cometitive tendering can be used for defined sub-contracts within the framework of a semi-turnkey of cost reinbursable turnkey contract. Along this idea, the turnkey contractor, having reached a specific stage of detailed design, could allow a specific amount of work to be let on the basis of competitive tender.

For the genuine turnkey situations, the World Bank guidelines suggest one path by which to facilitate the comparison of bids. The guidelines recommend a two-step procedure, in the first step, technical bids are requested describing the bidder's proposal for meeting the agency's stated needs. After comparing the merits of the competing proposals from a technical point of view, priced bids are invited in the second phase on the basis of a technical specification that at least in theory will make the bids comparable on the basis of objective evaluation criteria.

As regards general conditions, there is no difficulty, in principle, in insisting that bids in connection with negotiated procurement be based on a uniform set of general conditions. The formality of competitive tendering regarding submission and opening of bids may seem unwarranted with regard to negotiated procurement. Some measure of formality should be retained, however, and the relevant procedure should be made known and enforced. Furthermore, confidentiality could and should be maintained also in relation to negotiated procurement.

If bids are invited under the express reservation that the agency may wish to negotiate with any bidder, there is no need for the agency to reject bids that do not conform to the specifications. This is an important difference from the rule of consistency that applies to competitive tendering. On the other hand, consistency requires that the agency have the necessary authorizations and financial resources to proceed with the award of contract following an invitation to tender for a negotiated contract.

To sum up, it appears possible to conduct negotiated procurement in a manner that gives scope for competition, while at the same time respecting the principles of non-discrimination and objectivity. This method requires much skill experience and integrity of the procurement agency concerned.

9

IN-HOUSE INFORMATION UNITS FOR IMPORT AGENCIES

H.K. RAINA*

To assure that their managers base buying decisions on current market data, government import agencies should set up specialized information units. In a public importing agency the need for commercial information is as important as it is in any other type of business enterprise. Information can provide guidelines for each step in the procurement process, from the estimation of demand for a product through the final distribution arrangements. In many government purchasing agencies and state trading organizations, however, procurement officials have very little time to collect and analyze relevant market information themselves, because a large part of their day is taken up by decision making of various types, whether on trivial issues or important business matters.

*H.K. Raina is Senior General Manager of the Minerals and Metals Trading Corporation of India, Ltd This article is based on a study that he recently prepared under ITC's techniques cooperation programme in import operations and techniques, entitled A Market Information and Intelligence System for Government Purchasing Entities and State Trading Organizations: A Framework.

One of the requirements of a government procurement agency is therefore the systematic collection of published material related to the products that it imports. Obtaining such information is, however, only the first step, as the information collected often has to be analyzed or synthesized before usable inferences can be drawn from it for decisionmaking. This task can at times become very complex, involving the application of specialized techniques of economic and statistical analysis, operations research and so on. Because high-level executives and other operating managers have numerous duties to fulfill, they are usually not able to undertake such time-consuming functions themselves. It is therefore advisable for the agency to set up an in-house market information unit responsible for collecting and analyzing the relevant material. The unit can disseminate this information in readily usable form to those involved in procurement planning and operations.

Size and Structure of the Unit

The optimum size for an information unit in a government importing agency or state trading organization depends on the agency's procurement responsibilities. The larger the number and type of products it deals with, the more diverse its information needs and the more wide-ranging the research and analysis to be undertaken. The size of the unit also depends on the specific importing functions of the organization. An information unit in an agency that is responsible only for buying goods, for example, will not need to be as large as one in an organization that also handles, stores and distributes the goods.

Given the functions envisaged for the information unit, it should consist of two sections, one for reference purposes and the other dealing with research and analysis.

Reference Section

The functions of this section are smilar to those of a specialized library. They centre on the acquisition, storage, retrieval and dissemination of the information collected, in this context dealing with import operations.

Acquiring suitable material: An important task of the reference section is acquiring the required reference material, based on user needs. Users can be invited to make suggestions on the publications to be obtained. In addition, by making use of Guide to Reference Material (published by the Library Association. 7 Ridymont St., London WCIE 7AE. U.K.) and Guide to Reference Books (issued by the American Library Association, 50 E. Huron St., Chicago, III 60611, U.S.A.), which list new books published and carry reviews of these that have appeared in newspapers and journals, the reference unit can bring to the attentton of appropriate levels of management the new books that may be purchased. Many organizations find it useful to set up a selection committee for adding new material to the library, composed of representatives from different user groups within the institution.

Besides books, the reference unit should acquire technical journal specialized in different subjects of interest to the organization. Manufacturers' catalogues, advertising malerials and trade directories also form an important part of the collection. These can likewise be ordered in consultation with the procurement officers concerned.

If the management decides that it would be useful to subscribe to specialized information sevices in areas where normal published material is inadequate this acquisition task can also be assigned to the reference unit.

Storage and retrieval. In addition to the acquisition of material, the functions of the reference unit include the storage and retrieval of that material. Unless useful information is stored systematically, it cannot be located when required and may be lost forever.

Various storage and retrieval methods have been developed for commercial information. These can broadly be classified as manual, microform and computer based. Each has advantages and disadvantages, particularly from the point of view of costs and the level of expertise required to manage the system.

The manual systems include direct filing of original documents of copies and filing of extracted data on various types of cards. The growth of information and the need to economic on storage space has led to widespread use of microfilms and microfiche. At the same time the enormous storage capacity of computers, together with their processing and speedy retrieval capabilities, has brought into use large data bases permitting frequent and rapid access for critical decisionmaking and complex problem solving. With the advent of mini and micro-computers and video terminal facilities, the use of computer-based information systems is becoming popular with business enterprises in both developed and developing countries.

The system chosen by the importing agency should be one that allows the stored information to be retrieved or located quickly and cheaply. The choice depends on the volume, nature and frequency of use of the data to be processed, which in turn depends on the range of commodities imported by the agency, the volumes involved and the agency's responsibility for the various activities in the chain of importing operations.

The best approach for importing agencies in most developing countries is usually to start by operating a manual system that can be adapted for computerization whenever this becomes feasible. Computer-based system should be established only after a careful analysis of requirements and of the level of cost-effectiveness to be achieved, and after the consideration has been given to solving the variety of technical problems that such systems involve, including staff training.

Updating the information: Most of the information stored in the information unit will have a very limited useful life span. Once decisions are taken, based on whatever information is available at the time, they are usually irreversible. A large part of the descriptive information, for example, on who bought what and on what terms, is important for an impending import decision only if it is recent. Similary, much of the information on exchange rates, freight rates and even prices has very limited validity over time for decisionmaking. Because market conditions change rapidly, the information should be continously updated and old material weeded out.

Dissemination: Dissemination of the information acquired to the staff of the importing agency should, as far as possible, be tailor-made to the needs of specific levels of management. There are obviously substantial differences in the amount of detail required and the speed with which information is needed among different operating management levels. Dissemination has to be structured to meet these different needs.

Some of the information must be disseminated immediately if it is to be of value to decisionmakers. For example. Reuter's teleprinter service is useful only if the information is passed on to the import manager as soon as it is received. Similarly, other telex messages on market conditions need to be sent to users quickly.

Other types of material are disseminated onty after they have been analyzed, summarized, extracted and the like. This research and analysis function falls within the responsibility of a special section in the unit, described below.

Staffing: The staff for the reference section should have the same expertise as that needed to run a small technical library. Thus the person in charge of the section should have a degree in library or information sciences. He should be well versed in the practices, procedures and systems of information management.

Depending on the size of the section, he could be assisted by one or two persons. who need not have formal training in library sciences but who should have an aptitude for the type of work involved.

The training of the staff in the reference section should cover the following broad areas:

1. Role and purpose of a reference section in an import procurement agency, the principles of library science and its role in the reference section's work.
2. Sources of information.
3. Acquisition policy and procedures.
4. Processing: cataloguing (purpose and different approaches), indexing and access procedures.
5. Storage.
6. Retrieval and dissemination.

Research and Analysis Section

A major task of the research and analysis unit is to keep management up to date on relevant developments in the international market for the products of interest to the agency.

Although decisionmakers in government importing agencies,may obtain information informally through contacts with sellers' agents and other buyers and also through various newspapers, journals and other technial publications that come across their desks, the volume and the sources of information have grown rapidly in almost all areas of business activity. Furthermore, the day-to-day operating problems that come up claim a fairly large share of a manager's working day.

Thus, the research and analysis section can till an important gap by preparing such information reports as daily abstracts; monthly product reviews or notes; and occasional papers on long-terms trends in the supply and demand of products, structural changes in the markets, any innovative buying or selling techniques being adopted, major trade policy shifts taking place abroad and so on. If should also provide analytical support to operating divisions with studies in other areas that would be helpful in decisionmaking.

Daily bulletin of abstracts: One way to keep different levels of management up to date on market developments is a system of daily abstracts of relevant pieces of information from newspapers, technical periodicals. special, trade services and wire or telex services. The news, views, data and so an are simply collected and reported in summary form. The source of the abstract is given at the end of each information item so that readers can get more details on the subject if necessary. This type of reporting need not be undertaken daily. If, for example news from wire or telex services is circulated on receipt to appropriate levels of management, a daily bulletin of abstracts may not be necessary. The frequency of such a bulletin depends to a large extent on the flow of information into the system for the products and markets being monitored.

The person responsible for preparing the abstracts should have a thorough knowledge of the trading activities of the agency and should be trained to pick up those items that have implications for its importing operations.

Periodical market reviews: Apart from a bulletin of abstracts, the information unit should provide a monthly review of the market situation for each product purchased by the agency, based on a synthesis of the information available within the unit during the month. The report should not be too long. It should lead to a concise short-term forecast of the market situation for that item.

It is not imperative that the market review be issued on a monthly basis. In fact, for many products such as bulk minerals machinery, transport equipment and other captial goods, the market conditions do not change that rapidly, in these cases reviews may be prepared quarterly or even semiannually.

Similarly, the contents, the nature of the analysis and the reporting style will vary not different products, depending on the information available.

For some products, the reviews may take the form of occasional notes highlighting recent developments.

Product and industry notes: Apart from the abstract bulletin and periodical market reviews, it is useful for the unit to prepare occasional product and industry notes for the organization's managers. These notes can cover, for example, global trends in production, consumption, imports and exports for specific products over a period of several years. They can describe the structure of the industry, the major producers, main consumers, volume and direction of trade flows, and the like. The normal trading pattern (such as spot deals, short or long-term contracts, price trends, pricing systems and practices, and payment and other sales terms are additional areas that the notes can cover. Any recent developments that may influence the demand for and supply of the product in question can also be highlighted. A list of major world suppliers—names of firms, addresses, telephone, telex, capacity, level of production and specifications—can likewise be included.

There is a vast and growing volume of published literature on agricultural and manufactured products and industries. UNCTAD, the World Bank, the Food and Agriculture Organization of the UN (FAO), the UN Industrial Development Organization, (UNIDO) and a number of intergovernmental committees, associations and councils issue background papers and handbooks on most products and industries of significance. Depending on their coverage, these can often be used directly as notes for reference purposes. Usually they do not cover the names and addresses of major suppliers or manufacturers. For that purpose, other reference material has to be relied upon. This material will need periodical updating, unless it is revised by the issuing organizations themselves.

The preparation of notes, except of a very general nature, is a particularly difficult job for the product categories of machinary and capital equipment. Business enterprises usually differentiate their purchasing policies and procedures for these goods from those for raw materials and consumable stores, with the timing of the purchasing decisions being influenced at times by the tax laws of their country, which may allow tax deductions for expenditure on equipment for the purposes of renewal or replacement of old equipment; for the expansion or modernization of a plant; and so on. Apart from this, the selection process for industrial purchases is a complex one involving the assessment and comparison of quality attributes suitable for a particular purpose, which include such factors as economy, productivity, dependability, savings in time or labour, and durability. Because of the complexity of purchasing such goods, the buying decision is usually a group task. Quite often the agency may find it desirable to turn to an outside consultant for assistance in procuring machinery and capital equipment. A reputable independent consulting organization that specializes in this type of work can advise impartially on technical matters, recommend potential sources of supply and assess the offers of manufacturers. The agency's information unit can play a role in this process by providing background information on such arrangements by similar firms and on names of reputable consulting organizations. It can also analyze the agency's own past purchases and maintain up-to-date material cost indices.

Special analytical studies: Research is an intimate and continuing part of purchasing and of import procurement in particular. The research and analysis section can play a lead role in this function. In a changing international economic environment new developments in demand, supplies, technologies and so on are bound to affect the availability and purchase prices of goods. Threats to purchasing performance can be reduced by taking remedial action at the right time. Similarly, opportunities offered by new developments can be exploited if the signals are picked up early and timely plans are initiated. Preparation for an impending negotiation can also be an area of research. The section's scope for research is therefore quite broad.

Staffing requirements: The expertise required for the research and analysis section includes a knowledge of the principles of economics, in order to analyze information and present it in the form of abstract bulletins, market reviews, product notes and special studies.

In addition, the staff should be familiar with the follwing subjects:

1. Supply management: principles and applications.
2. International procurement techniques.
3. Import management techniques.
4. International market structure of specific products.
5. Sources and uses of information.

The emphasis on supply management and international buying is important, as without such expertise the staff may not be in a position to collect relevant information and analyze it in a way that makes it useful to management.

Relationships with outside institutions

Apart from establishing good working relationships with other divisions in the agency, the information unit should make professional contact with outside agencies. An important task of the reference section is to become familiar with external sources of information and work with them on a mutually beneficial basis. These sources could include public business libraries, commercial in formation services, trade and industry associations, chambers of commerce, public enterprises, publishers of trade journals, educational institutions, research organizations, embassies and international organizations. Most of these will have information and publications units. The person in charge of the reference section should make an effort to build up a close working relationship with his counterparts in these organizations.

The research and analysis section should like-wise develop a close relationship with outstde organizations. A large volume of research and analysis is undertaken by government departments, academic institutions, associations of trade and industry, international institutions and the like, which can help reduce the strain on the section's own manpower resources.

APPENDIX

THE IMPORTANCE OF FASHION IN TEXTILE MARKETING

BY THE IIC*

Styling and design play a strategic role in the marketing of clothing and textiles in the industrialized countries. In developed countries fashion dynamism is now perhaps the most potent element in textile and clothing marketing. When an exporter in a developing country sets out to sell finished textile goods in any of the industrialized markets, he must therefore face up to the make-or-break importance of the design factor in the manufacturing and marketing of his textile items. The more accurately his product reflects current fashion and styling, the more saleable it can become, and the better price it can command. Thus, through higher value added—in terms of greater attention to and investment in the fashion design aspect of his textile products—he should be better able to maximize his returns on each item exported.

The fashion phenomenon is by no means confined to the markets for clothing and textiles or even this generation. Probably every society above the level of a subsistence economy demonstrates changing styles in its pure and utilitarian art

*The International Institute for Cotton (IIC) is a promotional and technical research organization for cotton, headquartered in Brussels. This article was originally presented as a paper in a series of roving seminars on textile export marketing held in 16 developing countries. The seminars were conducted by the IIC as part of ITC's technical co operation project with cotton producing developing countries in market adaptation.

forms. Old people of any generation can think back over a kaleidoscope of changes that have taken place in their lifetimes in painting, pottery and furniture design; in the line of their motor cars; and in the architecture of their cities.

The phenomenon of such change is not new. There can be no doubt, however, that today's rate of change is very much greater than at any time in history.

Functional forces

In seeking to explain why such changes occur, is necessary to distinguish two distinct generators of change—functional forces and fashion.

Functional forces may be defined as those resulting from or required by technological advances of every sort, along with socio-economic developments which allow for improvement or diversification of what has gone before for, vice versa, which may prohibit the continuance of an established normal).

In the context of textiles a number of clear examples may be given of technological forces—the introduction of a new fibre arrow and better finish ing process, the ability to spin liner and stronger yarns, the reduction of kniting costs. All will have an immediate and long-term effect on the fabrics produced—and set new parameters in clothing and household textiles.

Socio-economic forces are clearly even greater forerunners of change. Perhaps the example most relevant to the subject of this article is the ongoing effects of the booming (swinging)' '60s. That decade marked an almost uninterrupted advance in wealth at every social level in the industrialized countries and the establishment of a new, greatly expanded and economically secure middle class.

The rise of this new group was paralleled by the introduction of much longer periods of leisure time for all, both in terms of annual leave, shorter working hours and, in many cases, the elimination of Saturday working.

Just one of the predictable outcomes of this new situation was the appearance of a new branch of textile production catering for leisure wear. This departure has had long-lasting effects not only on the way people dress on holiday and weekends, but in the office, at social gatherings and so on—effects which are still with us today.

Functional changes in textiles and clothing, whether the result of technological or socio-economic advance, can be characterized as long-term, often all-embracing movements affecting the totality of clothing and textiles, as well as other consumer-oriented industries. They are frequently referred to as life-style trends and may persist like the jeans and leisure-wear cults for two or more decades, *i.e.* until some social or technical upheaval brings about change.'

The Fashion Dynamic—Why?

It is within the framework of the situation brought about by the functional forces just described that the fashion dynamic operates. It is mysterious and arbitrary to some, but the source of profit to manufacturers and traders who can master it. It is a dangerous animal, however, for those who cannot. Fashion is certainly a major factor in textile offtake—the need to keep up with it means a higher overall volume of textiles sold in the world than would be the case without it.

Many different definitions of fashion in textiles and clothing have been formulated, some of these conflicting one with the other. Fashion is sometimes defined as the accepted style of the day for the bulk of consumers. However, for this article that definition will not suffice, and when fashion is referred to here it will be described as "those aspects in design of fabric and styling which are related to the desired self-expression of the wearer or user of the item concerned." (In this definition fashion is not exclusive to the top of the market or only to the wealthy members of society, but exists at every level in its different manifestations.)

Fashion may or may not improve the wearer's comfort or efficiency, and certainly it does not always do so. Nor can fashion be considered merely a tool to increase sexual allure—the effect of a number of historical as well as recent trends has quite frequently been rather the opposite—or its effects in this respect have been distinctly indirect.

In fact, if the idea of self expression is denied, the question arises as to why fashions chage at all. Why not save money and time by continuing with old tried designs until technological or social evolution call for or allow something different—more practical, comfortable, more suited to the activities of the people who wear them?

Trend-setters

One hypothesis of how the fashion dynamic operates meets most of the facts in the textile and clothing area.

Simply stated, it suggests that one group of individuals in society, the trend setters or innovators (frequently but not always the young or most interesting group—the people with bright futures and the security of both success or birth) tend to dress in a way which will differentiate them from those they consider not of their privileged clique ("differentialation" phase).

Next those outsiders who aspire to the ideals, glory or social position of the trend-setting group and who have the interest and resources to copy them, demand clothing and textiles just like those of their would be peers—probably from expensive boutiques and shops in the right part of the cities they inhabit (the "primary imitative" phase).

Soon even the relatively less concerned groups are demanding just the same thing in the mass markets ("secondary imitative" phase).

Finally, even those who have not the least concern for fashion—the so-called "laggards"—are sucked into the system simply because they either do not wish to look different from most of their contemporaries, or perhaps because they can find nothing else in the shops to fit them. Thus a fashion extends down the market and up the age groups in an overwhelmingly commercially important way. Of course the would-be innovators who started the movement off see what is happening quite early in the primary imitative phase and start doing something different, *i.e.* beginnig another fashion trend.

Thus, we can define a "trend" (in clothing as well as in furniture, food, philosophy, art and so on) as a phenomenon that is gradually being accepted by the minority of a definable group As soon as the acceptance level reaches the majority, one can no longer speak of a trend: It has become the acceptable average fashion. Against this norm, the innovators will react with new anti-conformist ideas which in turn may, or may not, get wider acceptance.

Multiplicity of Trends

Clearly the speed and penetration of the fashion dynamic and its ability to give rise to a succession of new trends is directly related to the wealth of the consumer groups concerned.

In a country of some affluence where all but the poorest levels of society can afford (if they wish) to follow many of the potential trends, as is the case in most West European countries, the situation can change fast and sometimes unpredictably.

There, fashion trends—until comparatively recently, synchronized rather closely to autumn/spring season collections in outerwear, from legendary designers in Paris. London and Milan—now come from all over the fashion spectrum. Fashions can appear and mid-season, although the main trends tend to manifest themselves at the two classical periods.

Furthermore, in today's many-sided society, with diverse groups of distinct ideologies, activities and interests, there may be quite distinct fashions expressing quite different ideas running at one and the same time.

In many cases this means that other parallel fashion trends are running concurrently but not necessarily in violent opposition. In fact, by the time they get into the mass markets, fashions which originally expressed quite opposite ideas among trend-setters are bought by the down-market shoppers, and worn without very much idea of their original "message,"

Antifashion

The antifashion phenomenon is a feature of recent years—examples might be wearing secondhand clothing and the "punk" movement. This develops in most cases as a reaction to the fashion establishment, and, particularly in recessional periods, the causes are not difficult to find. However, antifashion protest may itself become fashion when taken up by the fashion industry and accepted by the consumer.

The Vertical and Horizontal Spread

Fashion today is no longer confined to outerwear but affects virtually every textile item in the consumer segment.

The international institute for Cotton (IIC) whose promotional and trade servicing techniques for cotton depend heavily on projecting the fashion value of cotton in textiles and clothing, estimated in 1972 that some 50 per cent of all textile categories sold were to a greater or lesser extent sensitive to fashion changes. If the estimate was valid at that time, it now looks low. Certainly fashion sensitivity remains highest in the outerwear areas—the higher up market you go, the more important it becomes—but fashions now exist in underwear, and are important in all kinds of furnishings, notably in bedlinen. This is a phenomenon of the last two decades.

Other items also deserve mention. Fashion exists in such things as towels, dress shirts and even public service uniforms. Individual as these styles may appear at first sight, they frequently reflect the inspiration of the main trends in the outerwear area. Their designs are often much more subtle and long lasting moving beneath the high hequency outerwear fashion wave but nevertheless deriving their movement from it. Thus, for example, household fairs are once-yearly events, whereas there are many spring and autumn fairs for outerwear for men, women and children.

Fashion, Up and Down Market

Clearly, the supreme fidelity of up-market clothing boutiques to every fashion movement is of very great importance, as is a comparatively careful imitation in the more pricy department stores. Twenty years ago, the lower price, mass-customer shops and stores were either impervious to much fashion change or followed it only in its major manifestations and then after a year or more. Today a down-market consumer segment with money, time and the will to follow fashion more closely has brought the stores and variety chains into the lashion actoin much earlier than hitherto.

The fashion coordinator in the chain store is today as well informed as any in the fashion area. A great deal of the trading of that store will depend upon her decisions. In fact the fashion coordinator and her team will not only select as early as they dare the trends to follow, but in many cases specify the designs and the fabrics to their suppliers.

Commercial Implications of the Fashion Trend

The diagram at right of a typical fashion trend illustrates the importance to the would be importer of getting in early—but not too early—in the development of a true fashion trend which will in its lifetime, dictate the fabrics and styling in the volume markets. What happens at each point in time is the following:

Entry at point A means that the manufacturer can take advantage of both the early high prices and—if he has the capacity—of the bulk market volume which follows.

Entry at point B means that the better prices on the up-swing will be lost and his output will be confined to a declining volume market, and laggard purchases.

Coming in at point C is the unhappy fate of many exporters who have not kept abreast of the trends or have not reacted to them quickly enough. It will mean that their product ends up on the cutprice sale counters in discounts shops. Point D, of course, is not a point of entry at all, but a red alert for bankruptcy.

The Fashion Fad Danger

Of course the highly fashionable short-run producer—or indeed the well informed higher volume maker-up—may seek to go in earlier than point A, identifying a trend that will run its full profitable course so that he can get in at the price maximum.

This undoubtedly is a risk business because with so many trends starting off at the same of about the same—time, not all of them make it into the volume markets.

A fad is one such failed trend which is often characterized by a short and swift primary imitative phase and an alarmingly swift decline. The reasons for this are many, but the competition with other trends, the absence of valid values of self-expression, and the impractical nature of the product in use and wear probably constitute the major reasons why a fad does not become a trend.

Any exporter must take care not to try to beat the fashion establishment at its own game in the latter's home markets—or he must have developed his fashion information and design capacity to an equal or greater extent then that establishment.

Fragmentation of the European Fashion Scene

There can be no question that some trends do make it on a European basis—an outstanding example is the mini-skirt of the latter part of the, 60s—but even shorter-lived fashion trends will have a European dimension. However, caution must be exercised on a number of points, and the assumption can never be made that fashion in one country is the same as in the next because;

1. The fashion trend in the country of origin will probably progress faster in time than in other places.
2. The penetration of a trend will certainly vary from one country to another.
3. Each country will adapt the trend in terms of fabric designs, weights and product styling in its own way (not surprisingly, with so much climate variation in Europe from Oslo to Naples.)
4. A fad in one country may be a fashion trend in another, while quite healthy fashions in one country don't even cross a border.
5. Quality and size variations will be significant, even if the fashion itself is unchanged between countries.

The Outerwear Cycle

In a high production environment, a time sequence is necessary to ensure that the right fabrics are available in the qualities the makers-up require in the primary and secondary imitative phases.

Coming in too late at any stage in the market where fashion is important means no sale and is the second bankruptcy red alert.

This chart illustrates the succession of seasonal "cycles" from weaver to consumer. These cycles take approximately 18 months from fabric design to product retailing.

Decision-taking periods—at the levels of creation and development as well as at buying and selling levels—are indicated throughout each 11/2 year cycle.

In the chart, the texts above the horizontal lines describe weavers' activity, while those immediately under the lines refer to that of the making-up industry. The horizontal lengths of the "Fabric Fairs" rectangles and "Garment Fairs" rectangles give an approximate indication of the duration of the period during which important European textile and garment fairs occur. The same is true of the "Delivery to Retail" rectangles.

Example

For example, the preparation of the summer 1983 fabric collection starts mid-November 1981, at which time the weaver starts to create and develop his collection. Well before the international fabric fairs (which, as indicated in the chart, take place from end March to early May), weavers meet big customers who give their own design indications and place fabric orders for early delivery. These customer contacts may influence the weavers' creative staffs in their development of the collection.

The summer 1983 fabric collections are next exhibited at the international fabric fairs, for example, Premiere Vision (Paris), Fabrex (London) and Interstoff (Frankfurt); these are visited by garment makers and professional buyers from all over the world. The selling period for fabrics thus spans March-April-May 1982 and is succeeded by follow-up visits by weaver representatives.

Immediately after the fabric fairs, the makers-up begin to prepare their summer 1983 garment collections. However, big retailers do not wait for garment fairs to place their orders, but give detailed styling instruction to contracted makers up for the production of their own collections.

The period of the international garment fairs starts at the end of August and beginning of September 1982 with the specialized fairs for men's and children's wear (Herrenmodewoche, Cologne—SEHM and Mode Enfantine, Paris). These are followed by others for women's wear, for instance Igedo in Dusseldorf, Salon international du Pret-a-Porter in Paris. During this period (August-September-October 1982), retailer are studying the trends for summer 1983 and start placing their orders.

By September 1982 the weaver is progressing delivery of summer 1983 fabrics, the production of summer 1983 garments begins and makers-up representatives are visiting retailers with next summer's collections.

Delivery of the summer 1983 garment collections to retailers starts around mid-January of that year. Part of the garment production line is reserved for the realization of repeat orders and/or inter-season collections.

The consumer bying season summer 1913 starts around February and extends into the summer months, at which point the cycle is complete.

It is axiomatic that no seasonal cycle can move ahead in insolation and—as the chart indicates—both weaver and garment maker are frequently involved in up to three different cycles at their various stages at one and the same time. Thus, while from April-July 1982, he is performing follow-up sales and production of fabrics for summer 1983, a weaver's creative department must be looking ahead to winter 1983-84—and his factory will be in full swing producing and delivering fabrics for the previous winter season (1982-83).

Colours

Like fabric design and product styling. another important aspect, of seasonal marketting is colour—mainly, if not exclusively, lin outerwear and matching accessories, and underwear. Very early in any seasonal textile cycle, colour trends—typically presented on colour cards of great tonal accuracy—are researched and developed for the whole gamut of fabrics and fashion of each cycle. As the cycle progresses, some of the colours may achieve dominance to a great extent.

When the season is over many colours may disappear for years to come.

Conclusion

This brief look at the fashion industry indicates the supreme importance of fashion at the right time and all the way down the market. It also has significant implications when planning collections. For example, the higher the level of the fashion content in an item of merchandise, the smaller the volume required, as a general rule. However if the product's fashion component is clear and is accurately executed, the higher its retail price may be generating much more generous margins for the retailer and the manufacturer.

Therefore, fashion should not be seen as just a social phenomenon of developed societies but as a mechanism in trade to be mastered and exploied, just as an obstacle in production technology would be overcome.

APPENDIX I

PERSONALIZED EXPORT ASSISTANCE*

Under a scheme of the Israel Export Institute, small exporters receive assistance on an individual basis in approaching over-

*Nathan Hoshen is Director of the Training Division of the Israel Export Institute and is in charge of the programme described in this article.

seas markets. The Israel Export Institute has operated a programme since 1979 that has been highly effective in helping small firms export successfully. Called "Roving Export Managers," the programme is designed to lead companies to the export "take-off" stage so that they can market their goods overseas profitably on their own. The scheme, a combination of in-house training in export marketing and of field research and marketing abroad, focuses on small and medium-size firms with considerable potential for developing their export operations.

The REM Concept

A small or medium-size firm is often unable or unwilling to hire an export manager until it receives the first export orders that make such an investment worthwhile. A short-term export marketing consultant—in this case the "roving export manager" (REM)—can serve as the company's export manager in its initial stage of overseas marketing.

The REM fills an important managerial gap by guiding the firm's general manager in taking the right export decisions. He advises on how to make the first business contacts abroad, adapt production to market requirements and carry out actual export transactions. He also helps in long-term export planning.

In addition to generating export profits, the scheme serves as a training exercise for developing export managerial skills and marketing expertise.

Because of this training aspect the REM programme is administered by the Export Institute a training section.

The scheme helps firms that have never exported before gear up for production and marketing. These are two of the most important duties of the REMs. They often advise new exporting firms to odopt a "vertical" export strategy, whereby one target market is selected and studied in depth. The REMs stress the importance of concentrating all marketing efforts on one market at a time, to get maximum return on time and money spent.

The REM identifies buyers in the target market that are suitable for the client's type and price range of products. He also finds the appropriate distribution channels to reach those buyers. Again the channel selected must be suitable for the quality and price of the client's products, as well as the production volume of the firm. Small firms sometimes try to sell to large chain stores, which is often a mistake. Chains usually buy in large quantities at low prices, while small companies sell mainly in small volumes at high prices. Directing sales to small speciality stores through an agent or representative may, therefore, be the best way for such firms to approach the market. The client firms are therefore advised accordingly.

The REM helps organize promotional campaigns. He assists in preparing plans for participating in international trade fairs and suggests which media should be used for advertising the products. He may also recommend hiring an advertising agency to carry out some of the publicity activities and suggest possible firms.

Developing marketing skills: Also during this phase the REMs attempt to build up the export skills of their clients. For instance, managers of small and medium-size firms often lack knowledge of how to carry out business negotiations. Planning such business meetings and choosing the correct negotiating techniques are essential. The REM therefore works with the firm's manager in organizing and evaluating such sessions.

Likewise, the REMs help the firms write their first business letters in a foreign language if necessary. They sometimes recommend that the manager and his secretarial staff take the Export Institute's course in business English to upgrade their foreign language ability.

Financial support: At the conclusion of this stage, the REM prepares a proposed two-year marketing programme and a draft budget to carry it out, which he submits to the client firm. When the REM and the firm's manager reach agreement on the programme, the REM submits the plan to the Ministry of Commerce and Industry for financial assistance. Through its "Marketing Fund," the Ministry provides a two years loan on concessionary terms to carry out that programme. The loan covers expenses such as:

1. Participation in fairs and exhibitions abroad.
2. Advertising in various media.
3. Operating promotional activities such as exhibitions in retail outlets and training of sales staff abroad.
4. Opening sales offices and warehouses abroad.
5. Carrying out market research abroad.
6. Publishing product catalogues.
7. Registering patents, labels, commercial names and brands.
8. Using legal advice abroad.

The loan covers 75 per cent of the approved marketing plan. The maximum amount per exporter reaches 8500,000 a year, which must be reimbursed 12 months after receipt, in 8 installments. The interest rate is 75 per cent of the Euro rate. One-third of the loan is given in advance and the rest as results are achieved under the marketing plan.

Stage Two

During stage two all activities are shifted to the target market so that the recommendations of the two-year marketing pro gramme prepared in the first stage can be implemented. The firm can choose between the following three overseas marketing approaches:

1. A joint business trip abroad by the REM and the company manager to meet with potential clients. In this case, the REM and the firm's manager visit or participate in trade fairs, contact potential buyers, appoint agents or set up a sales organization abroad. As the firm's manager has been trained in how to prepare, conduct and evaluate business meetings, he can take an active part in the business negotations.

When organizing such events the Chamber is guided by the following principles; time is money, so schedules should be well planned; nothing should be left to chance—every aspect of the trip must be arranged ahead of time; success depends on follow-up; and business trips have nothing to do with tourism. Furthermore, for each event there must be a high probability that all of the participating firms will benefit immediately from taking part—otherwise participation is not advised.

Business opportunity meetings: Business opportunity meetings concentrate on setting up contacts for firms in special product lines.

The trade delegate arranges for the participating firms to carry on a maximum number of individual discussions with potential business parties during a two-to-three-day period. In addition, visits to industrial areas and commercial outlets may also be organized. The FEC covers the costs of rental of space for the meeting, an official reception or cocktail and 50 per cent travel expenses of the participants.

Austrian companies are invited to take part in such events through direct mailings as well as announcements in the FEC's provincial branches and specialized business associations. Austrian firms have ample time to prepare for the event and to establish contact with existing business partners in the market prior to their departure. This preparation is particularly important, since business opportunity meetings serve not only to help firms enter new markets but also to strengthen their existing business ties there.

About 20 such meetings are arranged annually in many parts of the world.

Trade missions: Trade missions have a broader aim than the business opportunity meetings. Trade missions are fact-finding trips that also serve to establish contacts with foreign government authorities. The FEC carries out such missions mainly to promote the economic and commercial image of Austria abroad. They are often the first step in entering new markets, for instance in Latin America, or in starting trade relations with centrally planned economies. The missions usually include high-level officials and top company executives. Such missions are often followed up by other promotional events focused on groups of companies, and they are always combined with business opportunity meetings.

In most cases all aspects of foreign trade are dealt with during a trade mission. As a rule, therefore, representatives of the import, trade also participate.

The delegation has official contact with ministries, chambers and the like, while businessmen in the group also meet with their counterparts in the business sector.

The FEC has carried out many such missions over the years to Africa, Asia and Latin America, as well as to various countries in Eastern and Western Europe. These events have proved to be an effective means of promoting Austria's trade. During 1981, for example, a total of 10 such trips were arranged with for following breakdown: 2 to Eastern Europe, 1 to Africa, 5 to Middle East and Arab countries, and to Far Eastern countries.

Technical-scientific symposia: the FEC's technical-scientific symposia are designed to facilitate the sale of Austrian technology overseas. This type of event constitutes a high level approach to information dissemination. A technical-scientific symposium includes lectures and films on new techniques and technologies and the latest developments in investment goods.

The foreign trade delegate in the market concerned makes all of the arrangements for the visiting group. He sets up the appointments, arranges for interpreters if necessary and organizes press coverage. He also assists in follow-up.

In 1982 technical-scientific symposia were held in Portugal. Romania, Czechoslovakia, China and the Philippines.

Publicity Activities

If an Austrian firm wishes to take part in overseas fairs and exhibitions, the FEC can arrange participation through group exhibits. The trade delegate cooperates with the FEC's Institute for Economic Promotion in organizing such participation and in helping out on the stand during the fair. The stands for such events are designed by an Austrian designer. The firm pays only a certain sum for the exhibition space and supplies the exhibits. All other costs are covered by the Institute. In 1981, the Institute worked with foreign trade delegates in organizing 67 such group participations.

The Institute also organizes special shows for Austrian companies in overseas markets. These are arranged for manufacturers of capital goods as well as of consumer goods in countries that do not have trade fairs.

The FEC refunds 50 per cent of the participants' travel expenses (excluding costs of accommodation).

An Austrian firm can also take part individually in fairs abroad, in which case the FEC gives it financial assistance towards the exhibition fee, as well as travel and transport expenses for particularly bulky exhibits.

The help firms with their publicity in foreign markets, trade delegates give them advice on suitable advertising media. Many foreign trade offices publish their own economic bulletins at regular intervals, and Austrian firms can advertise their products in them free of charge.

In addition, trade delegates help organize publicity events such as fashion shows, winter sports weeks and "Austria" weeks in department stores. For example, towards the end of 1982, a special event. "Austria Salutès California" will be held in the United States.

The FEC also refunds part of the cost of the export literature for Austrian firms, such as catalogues, leaflets, posters and audiovisual aids. The condition for providing such support is that these publications are in one or more foreign languages. Or, if they are in German, they must be marked "for export only." The costs of ads in foreign newspapers or periodieals are also party refunded.

Advice on Business Matters

In addition to the formally organized events and publicity support, the trade delegates help Austrian companies with their day-today business operations in foreign markets. For instance, they assist them in their discussions with foreign government authorities on investment matters. They also help them with such problems as collecting payment from their foreign buyers.

Gathering Information

Besides the task of searching out specific trade opportunities for Austrian companies, the foreign trade offices compile, analyze and update a vast amount of information on the trade, economy and industry of the country where they are posted. These activities range from gathering general routine information on new developments to carrying out special market research projects.

When a foreign trade office undertakes market research for an individual or for a group of firms in a particular sector, there is usually little or no change to the companies. If a group of firms employs a market research company to do large research projects, there is also the possibility of a partial refund of the cost.

Conference and Consultation Days

Each year the FEC organizes foreign trade conferences and consultation days in Austria during which trade delegates who are home for briefings are at the disposal of domestic companies to discuss their export problems individually.

As a general rule, trade delegates posted to countries outside Europe come back to the FEC headquarters for briefing sessions every two-and-one-half years for a period of two months, while those in Europe come back annually for shorter periods. One week during this time is spent on a refresher course in the Chamber, and another week is used to contact various governmental officials in Vienna. Then the trade delegates go out to different parts of Austria to visit export firms. These sessions in the provinces are announed ahead of time to companies through the Chamber's publications. For instance, a group of ten trade delegates recently returned to Vienna from Latin America for a two-month period for the type of programme described above.

Conferences organized by the FEC during the last two years for trade delegates posted outside of Europe have included those on Western Europe; North America, Japan and Australia; Latin America; Arab countries and the Middle East; Africa and South Asia and the Far East. The conferences take place throughout Austria. Consultation days, which are shorter and are set up for trade delegates returning from assignments in Europe, are held only in certain parts of the country. During the past two years these have dealt with Southern Europe and Northwestern Europe.

Services at Headquarters

All of the activities discussed above are coordinated at the FEC's headquarters by the Department for Trade Policy and Foreign Trade. Regional desks in the Department are the links to the respective foreign trade offices and also maintain a permanent dialogue with Austrian firms concerning foreign trade promotion. These desks also have an advisory capacity on bilateral negotiations and look after incoming trade missions, visiting groups of store buyers from abroad and foreign business journalists.

The activities of the specialized functional desks of the department are complementary to those of the regional desks. They focus on specific subjects, such as export credits and guarantees, customs policy, tenders, certificates of origin, the ATA carnet system and trade information, to name only a few.

Individual Services for Export Firms

The Chamber offers a tailor-made export assistance service on a permanent basis to individual Austrian firms. In many cases small and mediumsized companies in the country have considerable technical know-how, yet they are not geared to entering export markets. The Chamber therefore sends consultants to the companies at no charge to help in the following areas:

1. Product innovation, including advice on how to reduce production costs, improve existing products and develop new ones. A product innovation service was recently established for this purpose as part of the Institute for economic Promotion's wide range of training activities for Austrain businessmen.

2. Information on the latest developments in the world market for high-technology products, and new research and development work under way abroad. This is handled through the FEC's "Techinform" service, also under the Institute of Economic Promotion. With connections for international computer services, Techinform is able to supply, upon demand, information on foreign standards, new technologies and the latest technological developments abroad, or refer to relevant literature on these subjects.

3. Help with export problems. Export consultants, usually trade delegates on home assignment or at home for transfer, provide individual advice on export matters right on the company's premises. In cases when trade delegates are posted to Vienna for several years' time, the consultant develops a continuing relationship with the exporter and advises him on export problems as they arise. This service was started about 20 years ago. However, the number of export consultants has increased in recent years, so this service can now be offered to many more firms than previously. Local branches of the Chamber help publicize this activity. Notices are also published in the FEC's publications to let exporters know of this service.

4. Advice on market openings. The FEC recently started a computerized trade information service based on foreign trade data obtained from the UN Statistical Office. The statistical series show trade flows between different countries of the world by quantity and value. By the checking the statistics over a period of several years, and FEC consultant can indicate to a firm which countries have the largest and most consistent markets for particular products and where market potential has been neglected by Austrian exporters. These statistical reports are available to companies upon individual request, as well as through consulting sessions.

Training Activities

The FEC carries out various types of training in foreign trade for Austrian exporters (as well as for its own staff, as discussed above). It organizes and finances a one-year trade promotion course held several evenings each week in co-operation with Vienna's Economic University, as well as the Universities of Innsbruck and Linz, which is attended by young business people in export firms as well as students planning to go into export business, Chamber staff provide some of the lectures for this course.

The regional offices of the Chamber's Institute for Economic Promotion also sponsor a large number of courses on all aspects of export marketing and management as part of their general training activities throughout Austria. Lectures on legal aspects of doing business with foreign countries, transport problems, marketing, export paper work, questions of origin and, last but not least, foreign trade promotion, are included in these courses.

Export Publications

Providing published information on export markets to Austrian firms is another main function of the Chamber. The FEC gets information for these publications from incoming reports of its foreign trade delegates. This information is analyzed and evaluated in the Department for Trade Policy and Foreign Trade.

The FEC's information services division prepares a weekly bulletin, "HA-Kurznachrichten" ("News in Brief"), which summarizes important economic news from all over the world. The bulletin, published as part of the Chamber's weekly "Neue IW" (New Industrial Economy"), is a special foreign trade weekly and covers information on foreign markets. All companies involved in foreign trade can request a free subscription to this publication. The same applies to the special country reports (at present available for 160 countries), pamphlets on foreign trade information and market studies by product group for a specific country. Notices on trade opportunities, both export and import, are also published weekly and distributed to Austrian firms.

The FEC likewise produces a full-colour magazine in four languages (German, English, French and Spanish) five times a year featuring export product lines (for instance, sports goods, building materials and furniture) in each issue, which is distributed abroad by the posts.

In addition, most of the foreign trade offices issue their own monthly foreign trade bulletins for distribution in the host country. The bulletins contain news from Austria and advertisements of Austrian products, including photographs, based on information that is supplied by the companies. The foreing trade officer in the post selects company information for inclusion in the bulletin on the basis of his knowledge of demand in the market. The publication is distributed to the post's list of business contracts in that market. as well as to local chambers of commerce, profesional associations, the local press and television. For instance, toe office in New York has a mailing list of 6,000 names for its monthly bulletin.

Multilingual Trade Terminology

The FFC is involved in a special project to establish a multingual thesaurus of products and services. The project is being carried out through a joint "International Language Pool, "based on an informal agreement between national organizations responsible for foreign trade in Belgium, Denmark, Ireland and Austria.

The project is aimed at facilitating communication between businessmen and trade officials in different countries, for example to identify sources of supply for a given product. Work is under way to determine the terminology most commonly used for products and services in different languages, standardize it and list the terms systematically.

A Successful Experience

Establised more than 30 years ago, the FEC's system is woking statisfactorily, without any problems. It is financially self sufficient. Due to its very efficient information system, Austrian firms are usually well informed about foreign market opportunities and take advantage of them to a great extent. As all of the FEC's foreign trade promotion activities and services take into account the needs of the firms, the system is practically tailor-made for them.

Relevance to Other Countries

Austria's overseas commercial representation service has been studied by various other countries setting up or expending such services. For example, officials from Yugoslavia examined the FEC's operations about 15 years ago and subsequently established an overseas trade representation system quite similar to Austria's.

Some aspects of the FEC's operations may also be of interest to other countries. However, each country should study its own needs and capabilities to see which aspects, if any, might be relevant and applicable. Sometimes one country's experience can serve only as a general inspiration for others to follow.

APPENDIX II

MODERN TOOLS FOR EXPORT TRAINING*

ITC's Series of training packs and training materials in trade promotion provides the basis for conducting such courses in developing countries. A new volume in ITC's series of export marketing and trade promotion training packs has just been issued, Trade Fairs and Exhibitions. Another pack, Export Market Research, will also soon be published. This will bring to a total of nine the number of titles produced under this programme. More than 1,500 copies of the packs have been distributed since the series was started in 1975, and an estimated 10,000 persons have participated in training courses based on them. The packs are currently being used by 300 different

*Claude Cellich is chief of ITC's Office for Training Activities.

training institutions in developing countries and to some extent in developed countries. Some of the packs exist in several language versions, including English, French, Spanish and Portuguese.

The training packs have been developed by ITC in conjunction with outside training specialists to promote the teaching of trade promotion and export marketing subjects in developing countries. Training in these fields is of fundamental importance for upgrading the skills of the export community, yet such courses are relatively new in the curricula of developing countries' teaching institutions. By providing instructions. By providing instructors with a basic approach for teaching marketing and trade promotion the packs therefore help fill this gap. The teaching methodology outlined in the packs is geared to a developing country context, and each new pack has been tested during production to assure that it meets this criterion.

Concise Teaching Units

The packs cover in bound spectrum of trade promotion and export marketing subjects Several in the series are more general in approach. intended for new exporters and for trade promotion officials just beginning their assignments. Others are designed for business executives and government officials at the middle and top management levels who are already working in specialized export functions. The packs therefore range from introductory surveys of exporting and trade promotion to operational guidelines for specialized promotion services. (A list of the packs is given on page 22).

Although the packs contain the essential elements for conducting courses in these subjects; instructors using the packs some prior knowledge of teaching methodology, as the packs are not self-teaching kits. They are therefore not suitable, for example, for individual exporters who are seeking ways on their own to improve their marketing skills and knowledge.

Each pack usually contains three types of components: a teachers's manual, student material and audiovisual aids:

The course leader's guide gives background information for each session. An introductory session in the guide helps the instructor determine the students' training needs at the outset, while a final session gives a method for evaluating the course when it is completed and for drawing up individual action plans. Information on the objectives, timing materials to be used, special points to note and a synopasis of the subject are given at the beginuning each session. The guide also includes questions discussion points, exercises, simulation games and case studies keyed to each topic in the text.

ITC Training Materials

Name of pack: The World of exports.

Main subjects covered: Why export, what exporting entails, finding markets, the main elements of the marketing mix, overview, of exporting (15 sessions).

Principal target audiences: New exporters, trade promotion officials just starting on the job.

Material included: Course leader's guide, course members' material. exhibits.

Languages available: French. (English pack out of print but available on microfiche).

Name of pack: Export Promotion.

Main subjects covered: The need for export promotion, export promotion at home, export promotion abroad, organizing for export promotion (19 sessions).

Principal target audiences: Trade promotion officials, officers of other institutions involved in export promotion such as chambers of commerce and trade associations.

Material included: Course leader's guide, course members material, exhibits, cassettle tapes, game.
Languages available: English, French, Portuguese. Spanish in preparation.

Name of pack: Export Marketing.

Main subjects covered: Market selection, field research, product design pricing policy, marketing channels, marketing communications (21 sessions).

Prinicipal targel audiences: Businessmen, trade promotion officials.

Material included: Course leader's guide, course member's materials, exhibits, cassettle tapes, game.

Languages available: English, French, Spanish.

Name of pack: Export Procedures (Revised edition).

Main subjects covered: Overview of export procedures and documentation, transport and handling, prices and terms, payments and finance, the export office (21 sessions).

Principal target audiences: Exporters, trade promotion officials.

Material included: Course leader's guide, course members' materials. exhibits cassette tapes, game.

Languages available: English, French, Spanish.

Name of pack: Trade Information Services.

Main subjects covered: Role of a trade information service, collection, acquisition, processing and storage, cataloguing, dissemination, management (30 sessions).

Principal target audiences: Officials involved in establishing a trade information service, staff working in a trade informat on service.

Material included: Course leader's guide, basic handbook, exercise book, exhibits.

Languag's available: English pack out of print but available on microfiche.

Name of pack: Trade Representation Abroad.

Main subjects covered: Reporting, inquiries from home, sales representation, using publicity, helping visitors trade missions, management (28 sessions).

Principal target audiences: Commercial attaches trade commissioners and similar officials.

Material included: Course leader's guide, basic handbook, course members materials, exhibits issue the tapes, game:

Languages available: English and French.

Name of pack: Export Market Research.

Main subjects covered: Why export, market research, desk and field work, sampling techniques, preparing a research report (20 sessions).

Principal target audiences: Exporters, trade promotion officials working in market research.

Material included: Course leader's guide, basic handbook, course members' materials, exhibits.

Languages available: English and Spanish in preparation.

Name of pack: Export Product Development.

Main subjects covered: Obtainning new product ideas, designing the product, testing the product, licensing, protecting the product (12 sessions)

Principal target audiences: Exporters.

Material included: Course leader's guide, basic handbook, exhibits.

Languages available: English.

Name of pack: Trade Fairs and Exhibitions.

Main subjects covered: Choosing the right fair; preparation, implementation and follow-up of trade fair participation; publicity for trade fairs (12 sessions).

Principal target audiences: Staff in national trade promotion organizations, in chambers of commerce and similar organisations responsible for organizing trade fair participation abroad.

Material included: Course leader's guide, basic handbook, exercise materials book, cassette tapes, game.

Languages available: English.

Name of pack: Advisory Skills (Two volumes).

Main subjects covered: Methods of assessing a company's ability to export, using outside consultants (15 sessions).

Principal target audiences: Staff in national trade promotion organizations and trade development banks.

Material included: Handbook, user's guide, questionnaires.

Languages available: English in preparation.

Name of kit: Trade Information Exercises Kit.

Main subjects covered: International trade statistics, reference sources, acquisitions, classifications, scanning and subject analysis, cataloguing (20 exercises).

Principal target audiences: Staff of trade information services its accompany Trade Information Services pack),

Material included: Course leader's mannual, exercises.

Languages available: English.

Name of game: Tosca Carpets: An Export Market Research Game.

Main subjects covered: The market researeh brief, preliminary market screening, the market profile, market selection, report writing (5 sessions).

Principal target audiences: Exporters trade promotion officials working in market research (to accompany Export Market Research pack).

Material included: Leader's guide, briefing materials, various game materials.

Languages available: English, French in preparation.

Name of game: Devexport: A Strategic Simulation and Role-playing Game.

Main subjects covered: Planning of export and import strategies, negotiations with regional business partners, negotiations with intergovernmental technical co-operation organizations, developing skills to promote regional co-operation.

Principal target audiences: Trade promotion officials (to supplement Export Promotion pack), export execlutives and managers of state trading organizations.

Material included: Leader's guide, briefing materials, various game materials, information guide on intergovernmental technical co-operattions organizations.

Languages available: French in preparation.

APPENDIX III

SOUND MATERIALS MANAGEMENT TECHNIQUES*

Rationalizing import operations calls for efficiency not only in procuring goods and services but also in organizing the related materials management tasks. Efficient importing depends on more than just rationalizing the most visible aspects of import operations, namely, the acquisition of goods and services. Although in import operations the most attention is usually given to such matters as sources of supply, purchasing methods, escalating costs, supplier reliability, delivery delays and other related activities, the procurement of goods and services is only one step in a considerably more complex operation. The officials who actually contract for the supply of goods and services are dependent upon an inflow of vital information to guide them in procuring the right item at the right time in the right quantity. Getting this information is a by-product of materials management.

The importance of the many functions connected with materials management cannot be emphasized too strongly. The scope for savings is enormous—the outlay by a government or an industrial organization on supplies and equipment may account for as much as 50 per cent of its total expenditure. It has been estimated that in many developing countries as much as 20 per cent of the purchase cost of an item is lost through inefficient practices in materials management. Every step in the import process, from the decision to order supplies and equipment, through reception of supplies and up to the stage of

*Edward Henry is a senior ITC adviser on import operations and techniques. This article is extracted from "Basic Guidelines on Materials Management for Imported Supplies and Equipment," one of a series of practical import guides produced under ITC's programme on import operations and techniques.

ultimate consumption, is an opportunity to reduce expenditure. This calls for a high degree of professional competence and personal commitment.

What Materials Management is?

Materials management concerns the identification, organization and control of the materials inputs of an organization, whether it be a government department or a manufacturing concern. The principal activities comprising the materials management function are:

(a) Determining the quantities of supplies needed, their specifications and their delivery schedules.

(b) Preparing documentation to initiate procurement action.

(c) Receiving and inspecting goods on arrival in the country.

(d) Handling storage and stock control or distribution to the user department.

(e) Organizing stock identification systems.

(f) Maintaining catalogues of stocked items.

(g) Repairing damaged equipment.

(h) Verifying stock and carrying out internal audit.

(i) Identifying surplus and obsolescent supplies and disposing of them.

(j) Preserving stock and maintaining stores and equipment.

How Costs are Saved?

How does efficient materials management contribute to cost reduction. The answer is, simply, by ensuring that at every point in the supply line:

1. Stock levels are low and stock turnover is rapid.
2. A minimum amount of capital is immobilized in stock holding.
3. Surpluses and "stock-off," (depleted stocks) situations are kept in a minimum.
4. Stocks are subject to a minimum risk of damage and obsolescence.
5. Material resources are utilized as efficiently as possible.
6. Specifications are standardized and rationalized.
7. Capital equipment is utilized efficiently.

These are all significant cost-reduction factors, which can be measured to compare effectiveness and to assist managent in targeting areas of waste.

A Focal Point

Because of the widely different types of enterprises that use materials management techniques, either in producing goods or in providing services, it is impossible to give one single model for organizing efficient materials management. However, some basic guidelines can be provided for organizing the materials management function for government ministries or departments, although even in such organizations the requirements may vary depending on the particular situation.

A focal point or coordination department should be established for materials management for government offices, because of the wide variety of responsibilities implicit in this function.

One of the main functions of materials management is inspecting goods on arrival. The focal point can be responsible for ensuring that efficient materials management concepts are introduced by all ministries and departments responsible for administering the material resources of the country.

In principle the focal point should be involved only in defining areas and levels of responsibility; establishing and publishing policies, regulations and procedures; and exercising supervision of the regulations.

A focal point does not require a large number of staff. The organizational chart on page 7 shows a possible set-up for such a focal point (the procurement operations are not dealt with hero, so these units are not shown on the chart).

Maintaining equipment in good condition is a prerequisite to efficient operations. This chart is in outline form only. It may be necessary to expand the functions under the chief of materials management to incorporate a supply policy section and/or a section dealing with procedures. To a large degree this will depend on the extent to which parastatal organizations are involved in supply operations in the central planning process. (The greater the fragmentation of supply operations, the greater the probability of waste and inefficiency in materials utilization).

To which ministry should the focal point be responsible? This question can be answered only in the overall context of the ministry responsible for supply operations. In some countries the responsibility rests with the ministry of finance, in others with the ministry of works, while in still others with ministries of industry and commerce, ministries of trade and the like. In some countries the responsibility may be divided, with the finance ministry responsible for government stores, for example, and the commerce or trade ministry responsible for other aspects of import operations.

In general, where ministries of trade or commerce exist and have an overall responsibility for import operations, the focal point should be in that ministry.

Functions of the Focal Point

In broad terms, the functions of such a focal point are to:

(a) Advise the government on import programming and, where appropriate, and in conjunction with other departments and ministries, assist in establishing priority sectors for allocating available foreign exchange for imports of essential commodities and supplies.

(b) Develop forward plans for importing supplies and equipment.

(c) Review the present practices and procedures concerning all aspects of import operations and draw up consolidated guidelines for all organizations engaged in such operations.

(d) Review, in conjunction with the central tenders board or the equivalent body, tendering procedures and methods of adjudication concerning the award of contracts.

(e) Review all delegated authority for import operations and make recommendations concerning ways in which the government's purchases can best be aggregated in order to make purchases on better terms and conditions.

(f) Review procedures for stock-holding operations and establish uniform practices and procedures.

(g) Provide consultancy services to government departments and parastatal organizations in all aspects of import operations and materials management.

(h) Identify areas in which products produced locally may be substituted for imported items.

(i) Develop the concept of professionalism in the various functions connected with import operations and materials management, and assist in identifying training needs and developing training programmes.

Planning for Materials Management

Planning is one of the most important, yet one of the most frequently neglected functions of materials management. Sound planning of a country's material needs is essential to ensure that scarce foreign exchange resources are used to the maximum benefit. Planning also enables procurement officers in turn to develop their own plans, and warehouse managers and transport managers to anticipate future needs in their respective domains. A focal point should be set up for materials management for government offices.

APPENDIX IV

LETTERS OF CREDIT: HOW TO USE THEM IN YOUR INTERNATIONAL BUSINESS TRANSACTIONS

BY MICHAEL ROWE*

Letters of credit are a common means of arranging for the exporter to be paid for his goods. Some do's and don'ts on using this payment method. An international business transaction may be as simple as the sale of sacks of onions or as complex as the transfer of advanced technology. But at the heart of every foreign trade operation lies the same central concern: the supply of goods or services in one direction and the flow of money or counterservices in the other. When the buyer and the seller are located some distance apart, and when the transaction involves the jurisdiction of different countries, as in exporting, documents representing the goods, and the mechanisms to guarantee and transfer payment, play a crucial role in satisfactorily completing the transaction.

*Michael Rowe is a Paris-based writer and trade law specialist. This article is based on his recent book, Letters of Credit (see FORUM April-June 1986, page 39). @

Letters of credit, or documentary credits, are one of the principal methods of financing trade across national borders, and are often used by developing countries in their export and import transactions. Letters of credit are a relatively simple financing technique, provided that they are arranged in the right way. Particular care must be given to preparing the credit instruments and checking the credit terms, so that payments is made in the manner initially agreed between the exporter and the importer. As in other types of international payments operations banks are a key link in the process, working through their overseas correspondents and their international telecommunications networks.

The main steps in letter of credit operation and how they are carried out are discussed in the following sections.

How the Process Works

In simple terms, under a letter of credit operation, the importer asks his bank to issue a payment order in favour of the exporter from whom he has purchased goods. The letter of credit, which lists the documents that the exporter is required to submit to receive payment, is communicated from the importer's bank to the exporter through a bank in his own country. Upon presentation of the documents to his bank, the exporter is paid for his shipment. The documents concerned, which are a key part of the operation, usually include the following: bills of lading or other transport documents issued by carrier, an insurance policy or certificate covering the goods, commerical invoices, inspection certificates and certificates of origin.

There are many variations in the way that documentary credit operations proceed. But basically the steps are as follows:

The importer (the credit applicant) fills in a standard application form requesting his bank to issue its irrevocable credit (one that cannot be cancelled or amended without the exporter's agreement) in favour of the exporter (the beneficiary).

The importer's bank issues its documentary credit in accordance with the applicant's instructions. This constitutes an independent undertaking (or promise) of the bank and is enforceable against it, even if the importer cannot reimburse the bank.

The issuing bank usually asks a bank in the exporter's country with which it has a correspondent relationship (the advising bank) to notify the credit to the exporter.

The credit may be made payable at a bank in the exporter's country (the "nominated" bank) or more rarely at the issuing bank. In some cases the nominated bank adds its own payment obligation by confirming the credit. This gives the exporter a direct right against a bank in his own country.

The exporter ships his goods and presents his documents to the bank for payment. The credit may provide for payment to be made immediately or at a later date. It may also call for the exporter to present a bill of exchange (also known as a draft), which is basically an order to pay, as well as the commercial documents.

The paying bank sends the documents to the issuing bank and gents reimbursed. Often it is entitled to obtain immediate rembursement from a thired bank designated in the credit.

The importer collects the documents from the issuing bank and takes possession of the goods. He may have been required to make a cash deposit in advance with the bank or may have to reimburse it before receiving the documents. Alternatively his bank may give him a period of time during which to repay.

Some Variations

Letter of credit operations can be adapted to different types of trading operations. For instance, an exporter who buys and resells bulk goods for export needs to pay his suppliers from the money received on his resale (his export operation). If he can persuade the importer to provide him with what is termed a "transferable" credit, he can make parts of the credit available to his suppliers at banks in their own countries, and receive the balance—his profit—himself. In this way he avoids having to finance the deal.

Letters of Credit—International Rules of the Game

Banks all over the world apply a voluntary code—the Uniform Customs and Practice for Documentary Credits (UCP)—to their letter of credit operations. The UCP are drawn up and periodically revised by the international Chamber of Commerce (ICC). The main provisions of this code are summarized briefly below.

General Provisions and Definitions

The UCP apply to all documentary credits and standby letters of credit, and are incorporated by reference in all such credits (art. 1). Credits are separate transactions from the underlying commercial operations (art. 3), and all parties concerned deal in documents only (art. 4).

Form and Notification of Credits

Credits may be available by sight payment, deferred payment, acceptance or negotiation (art. 11). Credits may be revocable or irrevocable (art. 7). Revocable credits may be cancelled or amended at any moment (art. 9).

An issuing or confirming bank of an irrevocable credit gives a definite undertaking to honour the credit if the stipulated documents are presented and the terms and conditions of the credit complied with (art. 10). A bank merely advising a credit to the beneficiary undertakes no such obligation (art. 8).

Liabilities and Responsibilities

Banks must examine documents with reasonable care to ascertain that they appear to accord with the credit terms (art. 15). The issuing bank is obliged to reimburse an authorized bank that has honoured the credit, provided the documents appear to conform with the credit terms (art. 16). The issuing bank has to examine the documents within a reasonable time and notify any non conformity of the documents without delay (art. 16).

Banks are not liable for the adequacy or genuineness of documents (art 17), delays or loss in transit (art. 18), interruption of their business by force majeure and similar events (art. 19) or failure of other banks used to carry out the applicant's instructions (art. 20).

Documents

Instructions must give precise details of the documents required. Documents produced by modern reprographic or computerized techniques are acceptable subject to safeguards (art. 22).

Transport Documents

The transport document must appear to have been issued by a named carrier or his agent, indicate dispatch, taking in charge or loading on board, and, where applicable, consist of the full set of originals issued to the consignor (art. 25). A marine bill of lading must indicate that the goods have been loaded on board or shipped on a named vessel (art. 26). Postal documents must appear to have been stamped or authenticated and dated in the place of dispatch (art. 30).

Subject to contrary provisions in the credit, loading on deck (art. 29) and documents indicating a defective condition of the goods or their packaging (art. 34) are prohibited.

Transshipment (art. 29), "third-party" transport documents (art. 33), documents showing that freight charges remain outstanding (art. 31) and documents showing that weight or contents are not verified by the carrier (art. 32) are acceptable. The credit may provide otherwise.

Insurance Documents

Insurance documents must be issued and/or signed by insurance companies or underwriters, or their agents (art. 35). The cover should start when the goods are shipped (art. 36). The normal minimum amount of cover is the CIF or CIP value plus 10 per cent (art. 37).

Commercial Invoices

The description of the goods in the invoice must correspond with the description in the credit (art. 41 (c)). The invoice must be made out in the name of the credit applicant (art. 41 (a)) Banks may refuse invoices covering amounts exceeding the credit sum (art. 41 (b)).

Expiry Date

Every credit must specify an expiry date (art. 46). In addition, if it calls for a transport document, it should also specify a period of time after the date of the transport document for presentation of the documents called for by the credit. Failing such stipulation a 21-day period applies (art. 47).

Transfer

A transferable credit is one under which the beneficiary can request the bank to make the credit available in whole or in part to a second beneficiary or several second beneficiaries. It must be designated as transferable, and although it can be split up, each part of the credit can be transferred only once (art. 54).

Depending on the national law applicable the right to receive credit proceeds can be assigned even if the credit is not transferable (art. 55).

The above is a brief summary of some salient points. For the text readers are referred to the Uniform Customs and Practice for Documentary Credits (1983 revision, ICC publication no. 400). This publication is available from International Chamber of Commerce, ICC Publishing SA, 38 Cours Albert Ier, 75008 Paris, France, and through ICC National Committees and business councils. See also ICC guide to documentary credit operations and ICC standard documentary credit forms.

To take another case, a small-scale manufacturer who obtains parts from several different sources for a special export order also relies on payment from his customer abroad (the importer) to cover those purchases. If he obtains an ordinary documentary credit from the importer's bank, he can use this as security with his own bank, which can then issue letters of credit in favour of his suppliers. This is known as a "bank-to-bank" credit. It is important that the conditions of the two credits coincide closely. The manufacturer's bank commits itself to pay the ultimate suppliers if they comply with the credit conditions, even if the manufacturer for any reason cannot obtain payment of the first credit issued in his favour.

Issuing the Credit

A documentary credit is a highly formalistic instrument. Attention at the outset pays dividends later. The successful outcome of a letter of credit operation depends largely on the care that is given to preparing the credit instructions and checking the credit terms. In particular it is essential that the credit conditions tie in with the terms of the underlying commercial contract, and that it is within the exporter's power to produce the documents called for. The importer is responsible for making sure that the credit is issued as agreed upon by the two parties.

Unless the exporter agrees, the importer cannot change the terms of the sales contract by putting different or additional requirements in his credit instructions to the bank. The credit is supposed to be an exact reflection of the relevant provisions in the contract.

Suppose that the importer and the exporter hurriedly conclude their deal during the exporter's trip to the market. After the exporter's departure, the importer begins arrangements for the credit. When he goes to his bank to fill in a detailed credit application from, he alarmingly begins to think about a number of previously unconsidered questions. He hastily puts down what he guesses the exporter might accept, and sends off the from. The bank then issues it credit. When the exporter reads it, he spots something he has not agreed to and does not like. For instance, the credit may forbid transshipment, but nothing was said about this during the negotiations. The exporter then probably insists that the credit be amended before going ahead with the deal.

If, however, an exporter goes ahead and acts on the basis of a letter of credit that conflicts with the parties' original agreement, he may thereby demonstrate implicit acceptance of a variation in the original contract terms.

Application Procedures

The requirements for credit applications are laid down in the Uniform Customs and Practice for Documentary Credits (UCP). The UCP is an international code of practice for documentary credit and letter of credit operations, drawn up by the Paris-based International Chamber of Commerce (ICC). It has no legislative force but is applied by banks and accepted by (or imposed on) the other parties concerned throughout the world. The current version is known as the Uniform Customs and Practice for Documentary Credits (UCP) (1983 revision), ICC publication no. 400. It came into operation on 1 October 1984. (See box on pages 221-223.)

The importer is expected to tell the bank exactly what the wants. "Instructions for the issue of credits... must be complete and precise," states in part article 5 in the UCP. The bank's standard application form will indicate the information required. This includes:

Documents to be presented.

Amount and method of payment.

Beneficiary name and address.

Expiry date of the credit.

Description of the goods.

Details of shipment.

Whether or not confirmation is requested.

Most application forms assume that an irrevocable credit is to be issued. If a revocable credit is needed instead, the applicant has to give special instructions. If the credit is irrevocable, the credit itself when issued by the bank will state explicitly that it is such. If the credit document says nothing on this point, the credit is considered to be revocable (UCP art. 7(c)). (Under an irrevocable credit, the issuing bank and any confirming bank undertake an irrevocable payment obligation towards the beneficiary (the exporter). The undertaking cannot be cancelled or amended unless the exporter agrees. A revocable credit is one that can be cancelled or amended unilaterally by the issuing bank.)

Although importers should be as precise as possible when arranging for a letter of credit with their bank, they should at the same time refrain from burdening the blank with too much verbiage. "In order to guard against confusion and misunderstanding, banks should discourage any attempt to include excessive detail in the credit or in any amendment thereto" the UCP (art. 5) states. Importers have been known to insist on five-page descriptions of the goods being annexed to the credit. This is almost certain to cause problems when documents later have to be checked for conformity with the credit terms. An unscrupulous importer may request this deliberately to frustrate payment.

Making the Payment

When the exporter has shipped the goods, he presents the export documents to the bank and, hopefully, gets paid in return. Whether or not this happens depends on the care with which the credit has been prepared and the documents have been assembled.

The main document drawn up by the exporter himself is the commercial invoice, giving details of the goods and a breakdown of the price. Most of the papers that the exporter presents to the bank are issued by other organizations concerned with the goods and their shipment. These include transport and insurance documentation. The importer is assured that payment will not be made until the exporter hands over documents describing the goods and giving some evidence of shipment, although the guarantee is a limited one that does not go beyond the face appearance of the documents called for by the credit.

The exporter not only has to present the right documents but also submit them to the right bank within the time limits laid down in the credit. Every credit is supposed to contain an expiry date, after which it ceases to exist and can no longer be drawn on (see UCP art. 46). The validity period of the credit should reflect the time needed by the exporter to prepare and ship the goods.

The credit should also specify a time limit for the exporter to present his full set of papers, once the transport document has been issued. If he fails to do so, he is given a time limit of 21 days after the date of issue of the transport document. This requirement helps to ensure that the importer receives all of the necessary documents before the goods arrive. However, it applies only if the credit calls for presentation of transport documentation (see UCP art. 47).

Where applicable, both requirements have to be satisfied. The exporter thus has to present all his documents by the time of whichever of the two events occurs first.

Suppose that a credit stipulates that documents have to be presented no later than 21 days after issue of the transport document, and the expiry date is 30 June. Shipment is by rail, and the rail consignment note is dated 25 June. The exporter has to present his documents not later than 30 June, after which date the credit ceases to exist. In this instance he cannot make use of the full 21-day period after issue of transport documentation.

Payment Methods

A letter of credit may provide for the credit amount to be made available to the exporter in a number of different ways. In particular, payment may be immediate or on deferred terms, and with or without presentation of bills of exchange (UCP arts. 10 and 11).

Bills of exchange—commonly called drafts—are often used as financing instruments in international trade and are frequently one of the documents required in letter of credit operations. A bill of exchange is basically a written order by one party (the drawer) requiring another party (the drawee) to pay a specified sum of money to the drawer to a third party (the payee). In letter of credit operations the drawer (the exporter) writes out and signs the bill, instructing the drawee (usually the bank) to pay the credit sum to the exporter It may call for immediate payment on presentation of the documents (a "sight" draft) or on a specified future date or event (a "tenor" draft). A tenor draft is presented to the bank for acceptance. Acceptance constitutes an unconditional promise to pay the draft on maturity.

The exporter and subsequent holders of a bill of exchange can negotiate or discount the bill—that is, sell their rights in it to a third party, who then becomes the holder. Rights and obligations on a draft are largely independent of any underlying commercial deal.

The most common methods of payment under a letter of credit are the following, everal of which involve the use of a bill of exchange:

Sight Payment Credit

In a "sight payment" credit, the bank pays the stipulated sum immediately against the exporter's presentation of the export documents. The credit may also provide for presentation of a sight draft drawn on the paying bank, but since the draft is cancelled by immediate payment, this serves little purpose.

Negotiation Credit

Payment is also made immediately under a "negotiation" credit. In addition to the other documents, the exporter has to present a bill of exchange payable to himself that the bank negotiates, that is, buys from him. The bill is most often drawn on the issuing bank or on the applicant for the credit (the importer).

Deferred Payment Credit

The mechanism for a "deferred payment" credit is the same as for a sight payment credit, except that the bank agrees to pay on a specified future date or event after presentation of the export documents. No bill of exchange is involved.

Acceptance Credit

An "acceptance" credit offers a more popular method of providing payment on deferred terms than the "deferred payment" credit. The exporter presents a bill of exchange payable to himself and drawn at the agreed tenor (that is, on a specified future date or event) on the bank that is to accept it. The bank signs its acceptance on the bill and returns it to the exporter. The exporter can then re-present it for payment on maturity. Alternatively he can discount it—for instance with another bank—in return for an immediate cash payment equal to the bill's written-down discount value. Acceptance by the bank greatly increases the bill's negotiable value.

Conformity of Documents

Payment of the credit sum to the exporter is triggered by the presentation of the export documents to the bank. But those documents must tie in exactly with the credit terms if the bank is to make the payment.

The UCP expressly require banks to examine the documents with reasonable care to ascertain whether they appear on their face to be in accordance with the terms and conditions of the credit. The documents are considered to be non-conforming if they conflict with one another (see UCP art. 15). Slips of the pen or typographical errors may not amount to discrepancies for documentary credit purposes if it is clear what was meant and if the document is not rendered valueless because of such errors. Sometimes however courts have upheld a bank's refusal to pay on the grounds of slight errors in the spelling of a name or address.

The Transport Document

The transport document is the most important item of information that the bank has to examine under a documentary credit. The credit itself specifies the particular type of transport document required and any special characteristics it is to have. The importer and the exporter should ensure that these requirements reflect the terms of their sales agreement, and in particular the trade or delivery term they have chosen.

The main provision concerning the acceptability of transport documents under letters of credit are set out in detail in the UCP (arts. 25 to 34). These provisions were substantially remodelled when the UCP were last revised in 1983.

The transport document must be issued by a named carrier or his agent (UCP art. 25 (a) (i) and 26 (a) (i)). Freight forwarders' documents are not usually acceptable (art. 25 (d) and 26 (c) (iv)).

The document has to show that the goods have been dispatched, taken in charge or loaded on board (art. 25(a) (ii)). The marine bill of lading, however, has to be an "on board" document (art. 26(a)(ii).

If the consignor (the exporter) receives the transport document in more than one original, all the originals must be handed over to the bank (arts. 25(a)(iii) and 26(a)(iii)). This is aimed at preventing fraudulent dealings with negotiable documents.

Post receipts or certificates of posting are accepted if they have been stamped or otherwise authenticated and dated in the place of dispatch mentioned in the credit (art. 30).

Marine bills of lading and shipments by post are thus dealt with by name in specific articles (26 and 30 respectively). All other transport documents are covered by a general provision (art. 25) and are not individually named. These UCP provisions on transport documents can be modified and extended by specific provisions in the credit. The importer should give special instructions to his bank if the UCP provisions do not accord with the sales deal.

National rules sometimes restrict the application of these provisions. In India, for instance, detailed regulations apply to combined transport documents covering exports from that country. These include a requirement that the issuer of the transport document must have as his ordinary course of business the carriage of goods by sea as owner or charter of an ocean-going vessel.

Fraud

Suppose that the exporter presents his documents for payment, but the importer considers that the goods he has received are worthless, non-existent or not what he ordered. Can the bank refuse payment?

According to the UCP, "In credit operations all parties concerned deal in documents, and not in goods, services and/or other performances to which the documents may relate." The UCP also states, "Banks assume no liability or responsibility for the form, sufficiency, accuracy, genuineness, falsification or legal effect of any documents . . ." (arts. 4 and 17).

Fraudulent documents are one generally admitted exception. If the documents are not genuine, the bank has no obligation to pay. The same applies if the documents are genuine in that they relate to a real shipment, but there has been fraud in the underlying sales deal, for instance if old goods are shipped instead of new.

There is no concise definition of what is meant by fraud in letter of credit transactions. Cases in which the exporter ships worthless goods, forges documents or inserts false statements in genuine documents may all qualify.

Stopping Payment

Suppose the importer is convinced that the exporter has tricked him, but the bank does not accept the evidence he produces. To stop the money being sent to the exporter the importer asks the courts to order the bank not to pay.

Most legal systems contain provisions enabling courts to freeze payments provisionally until a dispute has been sorted out. Practice differs considerably. In general, however, courts are reluctant to exercise these powers in a way that will prejudice the independence of the credit contract.

In the United States, the United Kingdom and other common law systems, the disgruntled party can apply for an injunction, forbidding the bank to pay. The normal purpose of such an order in international cases is to keep the money in the country until the case can be heard in full.

French courts can order a "saisie-arret"—seizure. According to the French civil code, every creditor can seize money and effects belonging to his debtor and held by a third party, or object to their being handed over to the debtor, provided they are not immovable goods.

When the documents are presented for payment, the damage has already been done. What can the parties do at the outset to prevent fraud?

The importer can help himself by checking on the good faith of the exporter before signing on the dotted line. His bank may be able to give him information on the exporter, although the typical bank reference has to be read for what it does not say rather than for what it does say. The importer will be looking for the lowest possible pricing, and rightly so, but not if the price is so low as to cause suspicion.

APPENDIX V

HOW COMPANIES CAN IMPROVE THE QUALITY OF THEIR EXPORT PRODUCTS

BY LENNART SANDHOLM

Achieving the level of quality required for export products calls for coordinated effort among the various departments within an export company. It is opparent to most manufacturers that poor quality has a negative effect on profitability. Poor quality means costs for the manufactur in finding and rectifying defects. The costs involved in inspection, scrap, rework and claims can amount to large sums. Poor quality can also lead to a reduction in market share due to a loss of confidence on the part of the customers. It is not so obvious to many manufacturers, however, that possibilities exist to improve profits by systematic work on product quality, even where the situation is considered to be satisfactory.

Good results in improving quality will not be achieved through the efforts of a single department in the enterprise. It is necessary for all departments whose functions come into contact with the product during its development, manufacture, distribution and servicing to cooperate in this work.

Scope of Product Quality

The quality of a product is composed of elements that can be termed quality parameters. What these are is, of couse, dependent on the type of product. For a mechanical or an electronic product, these may concern performance, reliability, safety and appearance. For a pharmaceutical product, parameters such as physical and chemical characteristics, medicinal effect, toxicity, taste and shelf-life may be important.

A low level of quality in a product can be caused by weaknesses either in the design of the product or in its manufacture.

A distinction should therefore be made between quality of design and quality of manufacture. Two products that have the same use but are designed in different ways can be of different quality of design. There is thus a difference in their inherent ability to fulfill the intended use. Quality of design is evident in the specifications to which the product will be manufactured. Quality of manufacture, on the other hand, is the degree of conformance of the product to the quality requirements as given in the product specifications.

Who is Involved in Quality

The general task of an industrial firm producing for export is to identify the foreign coustomer's needs and preferences and then to develop, design, manufacture and sell products that fulfill these. Apart from customer requirements, notice must be taken of any rules and regulations that apply to the product in question. When a company carries out this general task, there are persons in many different departments who should be involved. They include staff concerned with market research, product development, manufacturing engineering, purchasing, production, inspection, marketing and service.

The role of each of these departments in assuring that goods of the appropriate quality are produced for sale abroad is the following:

1. Market research: It is necessary for the manufacturer to know what the customers in traget export markets are looking for. This is done through market research. For some products. the authorities in those markets may have set down regulations that must also be complied with. Information obtained by studies of this kind froms the starting point for the next stage of the work.

2. Product development: Personnel involved in product development and design are responsible for transferring the information gained from the market research into a product concept. The resources available within the firm, in the form of materials and manufacturing processes, must also be taken into account in this exercise. The experience gained from designing and producing similar products must likewise be taken into consideration. This can be done by ensuring close contact between product development and design personnel and their colleagues from, for example, departments concerned with manufacture, quality control and service. More formally, it can be done through design reviews.

The development and design work results in specifications for the product. The specifications must show clearly and unambiguously the requirements of all the characteristics of the product (including parts and materials). They must also be realistic. It is uneconomical to set out tighter tolerances than are necessary with regard to the intended use of the product.

The quality of the design is determined by these specifications. (See discussion below on specifications.)

3. *Manufacturing engineering*: Before the manufacture of a product can start, it is necessary to carry out production planning and preparatory work. This includes the choice of manufacturing processes, the provision of machines and tools, the preparation of process specifications, and the selection and training of personnel.

A precondition for economical manufacturing is that the manufacturing process must be able to comply with the tolerances set by the product development and design staff. This depends on the variability of the process in relation to the tolerance given (*i.e.*, the process capability). If this is not taken into account in the planning, there is a risk that additional costs will be incurred during manufacture (for sorting, rework and scrap).

The inspection of the product must also be planned and prepared. This activity is usually known as inspection planning.

It includes planning and designing inspection stations, preparing written procedures and providing inspection tools. Account must be taken of the risk of defects occurring and also the consequences of defective items going further in the manufacturing process or out to the customers.

4. Purchasing: The manufacture of products requires inputs in the form of materials, components and so on. These must be purchased.

Selection of vendors should not only depend on who has offered the lowest price. The ability to comply with the contract, both with regard to delivery time and quality, must likewise be taken into account.

5. Production: The manufacturing process must produce products within the planned time, in the quality required and to a level of quality that is in accordance with the requirements given in the specifications. Time, quantity and quality may come into conflict with one another. The consequence can be catastrophic if time and quantity have thoughtlessly been given priority over quality.

In manufacturing many factors affect quality. These include machines, tools, materials, operators, supervisors and management, among others. The way in which these elements influence the results must be known in order to achieve an adequate level of quality.

6. Inspection: Inspection consists of ascertaining whether materials, parts and products meet the quality requirements and, on the basis of this determination, a decision on acceptance or rejection of the goods.

7. Marketing: Marketing involves informing prospective customers of the product characteristics and the areas of use. There is a tendency on the part of some salesmen to promise more than the product can meet, which can lead to disappointed customers. The customers then judge the quality to be low.

In marketing, it is necessary to concentrate on the sector at which the products are aimed. Selling to a market for which the products were not designed entails a great risk that customers purchasing the products will be dissatisfied.

8. Service: Maintenance may be necessary for the product to work in the intended manner. Service includes helping customers with this maintenance by providing instructions, spare parts, servicing and so on.

Customers may have problems with the products The service department must be able to assist them quickly and efficiently.

Coordination is necessary among all these activities. If such coordination does not occur, there is a risk that goals of individual departments replace those of the firm as a whole, and optimum results may not be achieved.

Specifying Quality

Drawing up the specifications for export products is one aspect of this coordination, as most of the departments mentioned above should contribute to the specifications in one way or another.

The specifications contain tolerance limits on the quality characteristics of the product, for instance concerning dimensions of the product and other physical and chemical features of it.

Specification Limits

When setting specification limits for products and documenting them it is necessary to consider:

The user needs: These must be studied (through market research referred to above).

Requirements of the authorities: All requirements concerning the product made by the various authorities in the target market must be clarified (for instance safety regulations).

Competition: Studies of competitors products can be used in drawing up specifications so that advantages may be gained in marketing.

Process capability: Specifications that are not tailored to the capability of the manufacturing process lead to additional inspection measures and defects. Information on what can be achieved in manufacturing operations should be available to the product designers.

The balance between cost and value: There is a risk that the specifications may be tighter than necessary, because the product designers are usually made responsible for functional failures, but not for high manufacturing costs. A balance must be achieved between cost and value.

Clarity: Specifications written in terms that are too general can cause many problems and high costs. Care must therefore be taken to world the requirements in specific, precise terms.

Degree of Seriousness

A product with a measurement outside a specification limit means a product with a defect. Some defects can have serious consequences, while others may be unimportant. Information on these differences is required by those responsible for manufacturing the product.

By classifying the requirements (the specification limits) in terms of the degree of seriousness, and by including this classification in the specifications, the product designers can help the manufacturing and inspection departments to concentrate their work on characteristics that would have more serious consequences if the particular reqirements were not met. Specification limits alone do not give complete information on this.

The following list is a Swedish standard for the "seriousness classification" of characteristics. It has four classes:

Class 1: Product characteristics that are critical for the safety of the user.

Class 2: Characteristics that are critical for the function of the product. The function deteriorates very rapidly with increasing deviation from the specification limit.

Class 3: Characteristics that are important for the function of the product. The function deteriorates fairly quickly with increasing deviation from the specification limit.

Class 4: Characteristics that are of minor importance for the function of the product. The function deteriorates slowly with increasing deviaction from the specification limit.

The standard also contains guidelines for the manufacturing and inspection processes for each class:

Class 1: The manufacturing and inspection processes for the product concerned should be so designed that it can be assured that the requirements are fulfilled.

Class 2: The manufacturing and inspection processes should be so designed that the requirements can be fulfilled with a high degree of confidence.

Class 3: The manufacturing process should be well controlled. The inspection activities should be adapted to the capability of the process. Statistical methods are recommended.

Class 4: The manufacturing process should be directed so that normal variations can be expected to give results within the given specification limits. A minimum amount of inspection can be chosen.

Even if a seriousness classification of characteristics is not made, it is still necessary, due to product liability, to define which specification limits are critical from the point of view of product safety or which are required by the authorties.

Lot Resquirements

The specifications should also indicate acceptable limits for defeect within a given qualtity of goods delivered. Product requirements are of two kinds: requirements on individual products, and requirements on lots. If one or more requirements for a product are not fulfilled, the product has one or more defects and is considered to be defective. The number of defective items that can be accepted in a lot is defined by the lot requirements.

Lot requirements can be specified in different ways. One is the method of maximum fraction (or per cent) defective. Another is sampling.

Specification Documents

For simple products, the requirements for all characteristics can be given in one document, for example a drawing or materials specification. For more complex products, one document is not sufficient to specify the quality of the product: a whole set of documents is needed, which covers all the parts, materials, process requirements and so on.

To prevent the documentation going astray, a summary document should be prepared. This document, often referred to as the product specification, contains the requirements for the performance of the product, reliability, safety and so forth, either directly or by reference to other documents.

Product specifications should be laid down in a systematic and unified way. An outline for such specifications could be as follows:

Identification.

Relevant documents.

Description of product.

Product requirements.

Manufacture: methods and equipment; planning and follow-up.

Devlivery: packaging; marking of packages for transport.

Inspection: vendor's inspection; buyer's inspection; inspection lots; certificates; testing methods; initial samples.

Other stipulations.

Reference should be made to regulations, standards, testing methods and so on. These may be either internal or external documents. Both national and international standards may be involved.

APPENDIX VI

THE INTERNATIONAL SALES CONTRACT—CENTRAL TO TRADE TRANSACTIONS

BY MICHAEL ROWE

A contract is the basis for every foreign trade transaction. The main features of such contracts and some new developments relating to them. The contract to buy and sell goods is the starting point of international trade. Around the sales contract revolves a series of connected but distinct relationships, including the transport arrangements, cargo insurance, customs formalities and payment procedures. Although the contract is central to an international trade transaction, the rules and practice concerning such contracts may vary considerably from one export situation to another, depending not only on the legal system involved but also the type of agreement concluded between the trading partners. Some of these differences, as well as new developments at the international level to harmonize rules on international trade contracts, are discussed in the following sections.

Offer and Acceptance

An international sales contract comes into being when one party—the exporter—makes an offer and the other—the importer—accepts it. The offer and the acceptance have to match for the agreement to be formalized.

The principle of offer and acceptance is simple, but in practice it may be more complex. Suppose, for instance, that the exporter sends out his quotation on a standard from incorporating his general conditions. The importer then possibly accepts the offer. but sends his reply on a form referring to his own standard purchasing conditions. The two sets of conditions—those of the exporter and those of the importer—probably differ on various points.

Under most legal systems it will be considered that no enforceable agreement has come into being in a case such as this. The conditional "acceptance" in this example (the importer's reply on his own form) is merely a counter-offer that the other party may accept or refuse. But if the exporter reacts by sending the goods without mentioning the conditions, he has probably implicitly agreed to the importer's terms.

Form of the Contracty

In general, export agreement do not have to follow any particular form, although the precise requirements vary from one country to another. In many countries a legally binding contract arises from an agreement between the exporter and the importer that can be manuifested in many different ways—their agreement may be a formal document, a series of telexes, an exchange of messages between computers, a telephone conversation or simply an oral agreement during contact at a trade fair. In certain other countries, however, for instance East European countries, contracts must normally be written documents.

Conditions for Validit

Most commercial contracts impose obligations on both parties in the trading transaction. One party supplies a product (the exporter); the other pays (the importer). English law gives considerable importance to this simple merchant principle and refuses to recognize contracts unless they are clearly two-sided in this way. Lawyers call this the "doctrine of consideration." However judges over the years have allowed many exceptions to the doctrine that the exceptions almost outweigh the principle.

The doctrine is also applied in varying degrees by countries such as the United States and Australia that inherited the principles of English law (often referred to as the "common law" tradition).

Other countries, for example France and Italy, that modelled their legal systems on Roman law principles—the so-called "civil law" countries—do not apply this concept. However they have another doctrine that affects contracts: the theory of "cause" ("causus" in Latin). The general idea behind this concept is that contracts should enjoy the blessing of judicial recognition only if they have some serious purpose and are not contrary to the public good.

Many developing countries that inherited aspects of their legal systems from one of the former colonial powers are also affected by one or the other of these doctrines.

Trade Terms and the Contract

Export sales revolve around the movement of goods from one country to another. How to divide the costs and risks of carriage between the exporter and the importer is one of the most important questions to be resolved by the contract of sale.

Standard codifications called trade terms help to resolve this problem. The parties choose the most appropriate term from the list and refer to it in their contract. The best known of these codifications is a set of provisions called "Incoterms," drawn up by the International Chamber of Commerce (ICC) (see box on pages 245-247). The Swedish freight forwards association offers a variant referred to as "Combiterms," which adds detailed cost breakdowns to the basic ICC provisions.

The main trade bodies in the United States have recommended use of the Incoterms since they were most recently revised in 1980. However many U.S. exporters still apply the Revised American Foreign Trade Definitions of 1941. These adopt many of the same titles as Incoterms—FOB ("free on board") for instance—but interpret them differently.

The socialist countries of Eastern Europe apply the general conditions of contract of the Council for Mutual Economic Assistance (CMEA) for trade among each other. They use Incoterms for business transactions with non-CMEA trading partners.

Payment Under a Contract

Trade terms describe how goods are to be delivered, but they leave many important questions unanswered. For example, they do not say when ownership switches from the exporter to the importer, or when and how payment is to be made.

If the exporter and the importer do not deal with points such as payment expressly in their sales agreement, these questions will be regulated by the law applicable to the contract.

Owenership of the Goods

Transfer of ownership is frequently linked to the moment the risk in the goods passes from the exporter to the importer. In some cases the importer may become the owner as soon as the contracts is signed, although this is rare in export transactions.

TRADE TIMES

The terms below are based on the International Chamber of Commerce (ICC) Incoterms definitions.* The three-letter abbreviations following each term are recommended by the Economic Commission for Europe of the United Nations.

GOODS MOVING AT BUYER'S RISK AND COST

Ex Works (EXW)

The seller makes the goods available at his premises. The buyer bears the full cost and risk of loading and transporting the goods.

Free Carrier (FCR)

The seller delivers the goods into the custody of the carrier (or the first carrier in a multimodal transport operation). The risk in the goods passes to the buyer at that movement, and the buyer pays the transport costs. The term can be used for all modes of transport.

FOR/FOT Free on Rail, Free on ruck (FOR)

This term is for use in rail transport only ("truck" means railway truck). The seller delivers the goods to the railway. The buyer bears the risk of loss or damage from that moment and pays the transport costs.

FOB Airport (FOA)

The seller delivers the goods to the air carrier at the aiport of departure. The buyer bears the risk in the goods from that moment and pays the air transport costs. The seller normally arranges the contract of carriage on the buyer's behalf. The seller clears the goods for export.

Free Alongside Ship (FAS)

The seller delivers the goods alongside the ship in the port of shipment. The risk in the goods is transferred to the buyer at that movement. The buyer clears the goods for export and pays the transport costs.

*Incoterms 1980, ICC publication No 350, published by ICC Publishing, 38 Cours Albert 1er, 75008 Paris. France.

Free on Board (FOB)

The seller clears the goods for export and delivers them on board the ship. The risk passes from seller to buyer when the goods cross the ship's rail in the port of departure. The buyer pays the freight charges.

GOODS MOVING AT BUYER'S RISK AND SELLER'S COST

C and F, Cost and Freight (CFR)

This term is designed for maritime transport. The seller clears the goods for export, pays the freight charges and delivers the goods on board ship. Risk passes to the buyer when the goods cross the ship's rail in the port of departure. The seller undertakes to provide the buyer with a negotiable bill of lading that can be endorsed to transfer ownership in the goods or pledge them to a financing bank.

Cost, Insurance and Freight (CIF)

This is identical to the CFR term except that, in addition, the seller insures the goods against loss and damage at his own cost. The insurance covers the buyer, not the seller, since the goods are travelling at the buyer's risk.

Freight, Carriage Paid to (DCP)

This term can be used for all modes of transport including multimodal operations. The seller pays the transport costs. Risk passess to the buyer when the seller delivers the goods into the custody of the first carrier.

Freight, Carriage and Insurance Paid to (CIP)

This term is identical to the DCP term except that in addition the seller insures the goods at this own cost, for the benefit of the buyer.

GOODS MOVING AT SELLER'S RISK AND COST

Ex Ship (EXS)

The seller makes the goods available to the buyer on board the ship at the part of destination. He pays the transport costs and bears the risk in the goods until they are mode available in this way.

Ex Quay (EXQ)

The seller makes the goods available to the buyer on the quay or wharf at the port of destination. The seller bears the risk in the goods up to that point and pays the transport costs. The seller pays the import dues ("ex quay duty paid") unless the contract provides the contrary ("ex quay, duties on buyer's account").

Delivered at Frontier (DAF)

The seller delivers the goods at the agreed frontier, and bears all costs and risks up to that point, including transport costs. The buyer is respon ible for import costs and formalities, and for any transport costs after the frontier.

Delivered Duty Paid (DDP)

The seller delivers the goods at an agreed point in the buyer's country—the buyer's premises, for example. The seller bears all costs and risks in the goods up to the point of delivery, including transport costs. The seller is responsible for import costs and formalities.

In traditional CIF ("cost, insurance and freight") and C and F ("cost and freight") sales, payment is made against negotiable documents including the bill of landing This document is issued by the goods carrier and can be used to transfer title (ownership) to the goods. English law considers that title passes when the endorsed bill of lading is handed to the importer in return for payment. Most French court decisions have taken the view that ownership in CIF and C and F sales is transferred when the goods cross the ship's rail in the port of loading, but that the exporter does not lose control of the goods until he surrenders the bill of lading.

Reservation of Title Clause

If the exporter manages to remain the owner of the goods until he is paid, he can recover them in case of default of payment by the importer. Otherwise his only remedy if the importer does not pay is to take legal action against the importer.

The exporter has to reserve this right specifically—of remaining the owner until payment—by including a "reservation of title" clause in the sales contract, as no general legal rule exists to prevent ownership from passing until payment is made. Such a clause may also give the exporter priority rights over the goods or the proceeds of any resale if the importer becomes insolvent. However the rules vary widely from one country to another.

Belgian law prevents the exporter from using the clause against the importer's creditors. Judges in the Federal Republic of Germany favour the system of reservation of title and allow the clause to operate even when the goods have become mixed up with other materials. In France a law of 1980 gives the exporter using such a clause some protection in case of bankruptcy of the imporer. English court decisions have varied considerably, but in several instances U.K. courts have upheld an exporter's right to reserve a priority claim to the proceeds in the event of resale.

Because such clauses reserve special rights to the exporter, courts may insist on very clear evidence that the importer had agreed to the clause. In some countries, for instance, a mere reference to a clause of this type in a set of general conditions separate from the main contract document would not be enough for it to be recognized as valid.

Force Majeure and Frustration

Wars, revolutions, natural disasters and economic upheavals may stop an international sales transaction in mid-course. Large-scale contracts usually contain detailed clauses to cope with such events. National laws also cover this subject. In the United Kingdom and other common law countries, such situations are referred to as "frustration of contract". In civil law countries the usual term is ' force majeure". If performance of a contract becomes impossible, or in some legal systems unrealistic, the law will take action to suspend or terminate the

UN SALES CONVENTION

Many exporters and importers will soon have available to them new international rules for their foreign trade operations. The 1980 UN Convention on Contracts for the International Sale of Goods comes into operation on 1 January, 1988 in the following countries that have ratified or acceded to the convention: Argentina, China, Egypt, France, Hungary, Italy, Lesotho, Syrian Arab Republic, United State, Yugoslavia and Zambia.* (It is expected that additional countries will also become parties to the convention.)

The convention's purpose is to simplify the sale of goods across national borders by subjecting such transactions to a single uniform law. It will apply to nearly all such sales in which both the exporter and the importer have their business in one of the countries ratifying or acceding to the convention, or in which the contract is governed by the law of a ratifying or acceding country.

Contract Form

The convention deals with many of the basic procedures that traders need to know. For instance, does an international sales contract have to meet any special formal requirements? The convention says it does not. Oral agreements of various types, as well as written agreements ranging from telexes to formal documents, could all bind the two parties. However the convention has an escape clause permitting a ratifying state to insist that contracts with parties on its territory be in writing.

Point of Conclusion

A contract under the convention is concluded when either the exporter or importer makes an offer and the other party accepts it. Both the offer and the acceptance have to reach the person to whom they are addressed before they become effective. An offer can be revoked at any time before the importer dispatches an acceptance, and an acceptance can be withdrawn up to the moment it reaches the exporter. As a result, in the period between the dispatch of the acceptance and its receipt, the acceptance can still be withdrawn by the importer, but the exporter cannot revoke his offer.

*United Nations Conference on Contracts for the International Sale of Goods, 1981. Official Records, United Nations A/CONF/97/18.

However two exceptions exist in which the offer is irrevocable under any circumstances. The first is if the person making the offer (for instance, the exporter) so indicates, for example, by stipulating a period for acceptance. The second is if it was reasonable for the importer to assume that the offer was irrevocable and he acted on that basis. (The convention gives no guidance as to when such an assumption might be reasonable.)

Passage of Risk

The main point of an export sale is delivery of the goods. This may take place at any point between the exporter's and the importer's premises. Risk of loss and damage customarily passes from the exporter to the importer simultaneously with the transfer of merchandise. The convention's provisions on this subject are relatively brief. Standardized delivery terms are already widely used ia international trade and will doubtless continue to be relied on.)

The basic provision in the convention is that if the contract of sale involves carriage of the goods, the exporter has to hand the goods over to the first carrier. Risk passes at the same moment. If the sales contract does not involve carriage, the goods have to be delivered as appropriate at the place of manufacture or production or at the exporter's place of business. In the latter situation the risk in the goods passes to the importer when they are placed at his disposal in the exporter's business premises, provided that the importer would be in breach of contract by not taking delivery. If, for instance, the contract stipulates an ultimate date for taking delivery, the risk will not pass immediately if the goods are made available at an earlier date.

If the goods are to be taken over at a place other than the exporter's business premises, the place of manufacture for instance, the risk is not transferred until the importer is aware of the fact that the goods are placed at his disposal and the date for delivery is due. (Exporters will need to be scrupulous about sending notices that the goods are available and keeping evidence that such notices were sent and if possible, received.)

Trading During Transit

In some cases, goods are traded during transit. Oil shipments, for instance, may change hands as many as 20 times from the point of initial shipment to the final destination. In these situations, the ultimate buyer (the importer) customarily takes over the risk in the goods retrospectively from the start of the voyage. The convention, however, contains a provision that excludes this result in most circumstances. It provides that the risk in such cases passes at the date of the sales contract and not retrospectively, unless the particular circumstances of the case indicate a contrary intention.

Title

Other obligations of the parties are spelled out in some detail in the convention. For example, apart from delivering the goods physically, the exporter has to transfer title (ownership) to them. The methods by which title may be transferred are left to national law. Under some laws the mere conclusion of a sales contract may of itself transfer title.

Nature of the Goods

The exporter has to provide goods that accord with the contract specifications. They must be fit for their normal purpose and for any particular purpose made known to the exporter.

Default

The importer must pay the price and take delivery of the merchandise. He must then examine the goods promptly and give the exporter notice of any defects in the goods within a reasonable time. If the goods are defective or do not comply with the contract requirements, the importer can call on the exporter to put right the defect. Or the importer can unilaterally reduce the price or set an additional period for fulfilling the terms of the contract. If the defect amounts to a fundamental breach, the importer may demand that the goods be replaced by substitute merchandise. A breach is fundamental if it deprives the injured party (the importer) of what he was entitled to expect under the contract and it was foreseeable by the exporter that the breach would occur. The importer may withdraw from the contract for fundamental breach or for non-delivery if he has set an additional time limit for performance and the exporter has not sent the goods. The importer can claim damages for loss.

The exporter's remedies for default of the importer, are similar. He can require the importer to pay the price, take delivery or perform any other obligation, or set an additional period for performance. He can withdraw from the contract in case of fundamental breach by the importer, or if the importer fails to pay or take delivery with an additional period that the exporter has allowed him.

Damages and interest on any sum in arrears can also be claimed. Either party is exempted from paying damages if his failure to perform his obligations under the contract was caused by a factor beyond his control.

Application

The covention applies automatically to all international sales contracts between parties in the countries that have ratified or acceded to the convention. However if in a particular export trasanction, an exporter and an importer wish to write their own contract terms, instead of applying the convention, they may do so by explicit agreement.

---

contract and sort out the rights and obligations of each party. Normally the events concerned must be external to the party involved and of such a nature that the parties could not have foreseen them in the ordinary course of things, in order to qualify as "force majeure" or "frustration of contract". (The International Chamber of Commerce offers model contract clauses on force majeure and hardship.)

In some countries—the Federal Republic of Germany and Egypt for instance—the judge can modify the terms of a contract that has run into difficulties and produce a revised arrangement that is fair to both parties. But courts in relatively few countries have this power, although some long-term contracts contain hardship clauses that provide for renegotiation of the contract terms if the economic foundations of the transaction change radically.

All legal systems agree on one point: Only in exceptional circumstances will parties be relieved of their obligations under a contract. When the Suez Canal was closed in 1956, for instance, the House of Lords, the United Kingdom's highest appeal court, held that closure of the canal did not cancel sales contracts just because the goods would have to be shipped around the Cape of Good Hope instead of going through the canal.

To take another example, several years ago an exporter of steel thought he no longer had to deliver an order to a foreign buyer when his government issued a circular forbidding steel exports. The sales contract for that particular order contained an arbitration clause, and the importer initiated arbitration proceedings. The arbitrator found that the circular was not legally binding and that accordingly the exporter was not relieved of his duty to deliver. He awarded damages of £1 million to the importer.

Another case is import licenses. Often failure to obtain an import or export license is not accepted as a reason to break a contract, particularly if the contract does not mention licenses at all. The assumption may then be that each party has implicity accepted responsibility for obtaining the permissions he needs.

Companies doing business with state trading organizations need to remember that legally the organization is a separate entity from the government, which may have implications for sales contracts. If the government takes an action that hinders completion of an export contract, for instance banning exports of a certain commodity after a crop failure, the state trading organization may be able to use force majeure successfully as a defense for non-delivery.

Applicable Law for Contracts

No universally applied system of uniform international laws exists by which international trade transactions can be governed. (However see the discussion below on the UN sales convention.) Nor are there any international business courts to hear disputes arising from such transactions. Accordingly most international sales contracts are still subject to national laws.

The contract itself may contain a choice of law clause, stating whose legal system applies. Many agreements involving parties from more than one country, however, are silent on this point. If a dispute arises, the judge has to determine which legal system applies to the contract.

Each country has developed its own rules to guide the judge's decision on this question. These are called "conflict of law" rules or "private international law". The latter expression is particularly confusing, since both the legal rules applied to select the law and the law chosen are national laws. Only the dispute is international.

Factors that may be taken into account in deciding which legal system applies include the place where the contract was concluded and the residence of the parties. The current tendency is to apply the law of the country with which the agreement is most closely connected—sometime referred to as the "proper law" of the contract. Often this is held to be the place where the contract has to be carried out, that is, the location of the transfer (delivery) of the merchandise. In the case of export sales this is usually the exporter's country—the contract is performed (fulfilled) when responsibility for the goods passes from the exporter to the importer, and the trade terms most frequently included in sales contracts provide for this to happen when the goods are loaded on board ship or handed over to a carrier in the exporter's country.

If the importer and the exporter wish to avoid going to national courts in case a dispute arises over their transaction, they can agree in their contract to submit any such conflict to a neutral arbitrator instead.

International Conventions on Contracts

Although, as mentioned above, there is no universally accepted system of international trade law, some international law-making has nonetheless taken place concerning contracts for international trade transactions.

Uniform rules to determine the national law applicable to export contracts are set out in a convention drawn up in 1955 (called the Convention on the Law Applicable to International Sales of Goods) and amended in 1985. This instrument is the work of an organization called the Hague Conference for Private International Law. But few countries have ratified the convention.

A 1980 agreement adopted under the auspices of the United Nations Commission on International Trade Law (UNCITRAL) is more ambitious. It aims at providing a single system of law for all international sale of goods agreements. Its provisions are designed to replace different national laws and not merely to determine which national law applies. The measure will enter into force in ratifying states on 1 January, 1988 (see box on pages 249-252).

Eight countries already apply a uniform system for international sales contained in two conventions concluded in 1964, the Uniform Law on the International Sale of Goods and the Uniform Law on the Formation of Contracts for the Interntional Sale of Goods. (They are deposited with the Government of the Netherlands.)

The authors of the later UN convention referred to above believe that their own work will obtain wider acceptance and ultimately replace the two 1964 measures.

APPENDIX VII

PRODUCT MARKETING PROGRAMMES—AN INSTRUMENT FOR EFFECTIVE TRADE PROMOTION

By Camilo Jaramillo

Marketing programmes focused on specific products and target markets can be a cost-effective way to improve a country's export performance. Product and market-otiented export promotion programmes are one of the most useful tools at the disposal of a trade promotion organization (TPO) for expanding and diversifying exports. Such programmes are precise strategies for promoting specific products on selected markets. They outline the actions required to increase sales and the organizations responsible for undertaking each activity. The development and implementation of such programmes can help assure that a TPO's resources are used to the best advantage by focusing on the most promising export products and markets. Business and governmental organizations should be closely associated with the TPO in drawing up and operating such programmes to achieve the best export results.

Preparations for Programme Planning

To make the best use of its limited human and financial resources, a TPO should reduce its list of target products to be promoted through a successive selection process, until it arrives at the most promising items.

Preliminary Product Selection

A broad preliminary selection of products can usually be made on the basis of guidelines contained in the national economic development policy. The national development plan and sectoral economic policies generally give information that helps identify priority products or groups of products. Meetings with the ministries of planning, agriculture, industry, commerce and finance may provide leads on activities that are being or will be implemented for different product groups: these products should be considered when drawing up the list.

In the preliminary phase, available statistics on production, domestic consumption and exports can also be consulted to indicate export supply trends by sector, or even by product. Unfortunately, however, in many countries these statistics are published too late or are too general to be useful for this purpose.

An important factor to consider in drawing up a tentative list of products is current and future sales possibilities in foreign markets. Local products unknown abroad that would require intensive product adaptation and promotional efforts to achieve sales might be eliminated at the outset, depending on the trade promotion funds available. The TPO may also decide to eliminate:

Products for which raw materials are unavailable locally and that are low in added value.

Articles manufactured by only a small number of companies and thereby not justifying a joint export promotion programme.

Items produced principally by large companies with export experience and requiring little export assistance.

Export products controlled by specialized and well organized international trading companies, such as is the case for many commodities.

This process will give an initial list that can be narrowed down later for a final selection.

Export Supply Survey

The next level of selection can be made on the basis of an export supply survey, which is the most important step in formulating a product-oriented export promotion progrrmme. An export supply survey has three main objectives:

Choose priority export products and estimate the quantities available for export, at present as well as over the short and medium term.

Identify and select producers and exporters of those product groups.

Determine obstacles to exporting these products.

The selection of companies and products during this phase should focus first on companies. This is because it is generally more difficult and time consuming to assist a weak company than a well managed company, even if the latter has products that may still require some development for international trading. The companies should be selected according to certain criteria, such as:

The firm's managerial capacity.

The export motivation of its managers.

Idle production capacity of the plant.

Availability of raw materials to produce the company's products.

This information can be obtained through company questionnaires. TPO staff should, in principle, visit individual companies to complete the questionnaires. When the number of companies is quite large, it is better to conduct the survey sector by sector than to resort to an overall survey by mail. The TPO official doing the interviews should be the product manager for the particular items concerned. This will also allow the TPO to get precise knowledge of the industry as a whole. The interviewer should request to visit the company premises, which can help in assessing the production facilities.

The quality and the reliability of the answers obtained through the interviews will depend to a great extent on the businessmen's confidence in the interviewer. It is therefore essential that the interviewers be technically knowledgeable. In some cases it may be advisable for business associations (such as chambers of commerce or professional associations) to assist in preparing the questionnaire and in the interviewing. This can help create a climate of confidence.

The export supply survey should result in a clear picture of the characteristics and volume of the existing products that are available for export from the country, as well as of the product development possibilities, that is, the type and volume of other goods that could be adapted for export or produced if there is foreign demand for them. The firms producing those products should also clearly emerge from the survey. At the same time, the type of inputs required for product adaptation and new production should result from the exercise.

An export supply survey must be updated periodically. Contact must therefore be renewed with the same businessmen approximately every two years. To maintain their goodwill, it is essential that the TPO and the private association participating inform all companies interviewed about the main findings of the survey and how the information collected is to be used.

Grouping the Products

The tentative list of priority products initially drawn up can be further refined as a result of the supply survey. The products produced by the most promising companies can be listed and separated into groups. The groups can be drawn up so that items with similar export marketing characteristics are together, such as common marketing channels. For example, most canned vegetables or fruits can be considered as one group.

It may be necessary to restrict the number of groups of products if the list is quite long. Two of the most common criteria for determining priority products are the number of companies concerned and the volume of supply available for export. Consideration must likewise be given to national industrial, agricultural and foreign trade policies, as mentioned above.

Demand Studies

The TPO must then undertake international demand studies on the tentative list of product groups, comparing sales prospects with the supply identified in the preceding phase. Market profiles drawn up by commercial attaches abroad can be used as background for this exercise. These surveys usually consist of two stages: preliminary desk research for basic statistical data and information, and field research for more detailed information, particularly on such matters as the price structure, competition and consumer preferences. Adequate funds must of course be allocated for field research. The demand analysis should cover not only customers' current requirements but also potential demand.

Final Product List

On the basis of the demand studies, a final list of products can be drawn up. The final list should cover product group that have confirmed export potential, as demonstrated in the demand studies. The selection should also partly be determined by the ability of the TPO to implement the appropriate export promotion programmes for the items in question.

For large product categories, companies can be grouped by size, export experience, possibilities of export expansion, total turnover and so on.

Selecting Markets

The list of target markets for the promotional programmes can be drawn up as a result of the demand studies. A preliminary list of target markets can be based on the volume of imports and import trends for the priority product groups. Negative factors concerning market access should also be considered in this general review. Any market that will demand an excessive marketing effort to achieve sales should be dropped.

It will next be necessary to do more in-depth market research to arrive at a final list of markets. This research can be carried out with the close cooperation of the commercial attaches or equivalent trade promotion staff abroad, among other available sources. Factors that should be examined in detail at this stage are import tariffs and regulations; the existence of any tariff preferences, and of tariff and non-tariff barriers; the prevailing price levels; buyers' requirements; competitive products imported into that market; promotional activities of competitors; and so forth. This research should lead to a clear indication of which markets offer the best possibilities for market penetration of the selected products.

Drawing up Individual Marketing Plans

For each product group, the TPO should next draw up a programme to remove or reduce any export constraints identified in the export supply survey and to define export promotion activities. No export promotion activities should be undertaken if the obstacles to successful exporting cannot be eliminated in the short term.

Working Group

The work carried out so far will have been performed mainly by the TPO's product managers, except for the possible participation of business associations in the interview process and of the commercial attaches in supplying market information. However, the active participation of a number of other people not directly connected with the TPO will be necessary for drawing up the individual marketing plans. This participation will be essential, since the TPO's role is mainly catalytical, whereas the other parties involved will be directly responsible for executing most of the activities.

A selection of producers and exporters (between six and nine) should be invited to participate in drawing up the different product marketing plans. Leading exporters of the product should be included, to benefit from their marketing experience, and also small and medium-size exporters, to get a direct knowledge of the types of problems they face and to include in the marketing plan specific actions to deal with those problems. It should be clear to both the participants and the firms not directly involved in drawing up the plan that the marketing plan will be for the use of the industry as a whole. Non-participants can make their voices heard either through direct communication or through sectoral associations.

In addition to producers and exporters, others who should be involved in developing the individual product marketing plans are suppliers of important raw materials to be used in the export product; certain services such as banking, insurance and transportation; and a number of official bodies that can affect in one way or another the export performance in that product group, including certain ministries concerned with production aspects or that have an important role in fiscal matters.

As a general rule, it is advisable to limit the working group for each product category to 15 participants, including the corresponding TPO product manager, who should be the leader of the group.

Features of the Marketing Plans

Each marketing plan should:

Specify the target markets for the product(s) in question, based on the market selection process described above. The marketing plan should concentrate on a limited number of target markets.

Set export targets in value terms for each market on the basis of the estimated supply and demand, together with an indication of the tentative time schedule for their achievement. The targets should be realistic but ambitious. In other words, they should imply substantial efforts from the producers concerned. At the same time they should take into account the degree of support expected from the relevant authorities to carry out the marketing plan.

Outline the export development and promotional activities required. Once the markets have been selected and export targets have been established, the next step is to give details on the specific activities to be undertaken. Some examples of export development activities are redesigning the products to comply with foreign buyers' tastes, adapting, labelling to market regulations and expanding output certain articles in high demand. Promotion activities are also required.

Identify the private or public organizations and/or companies that can contribute to, or be made responsible for, implementing each of the above activities.

The costs for carrying out the activities foreseen should be estimated for each marketing plan.

Individual Activity Work Plans

Each activity within the overall plan must next be presented in detail in a separate work plan containing the following:

1. Title and objective of the activity; description of the activity.

2. Participating (benefitting) companies.

3. Tentative list of implementing organizations.

4. Programme of action.

A. By step: description of each step, names of implementing organizations, estimated duration of each step, actual duration of each step (to be filled in later), remarks (to be given on completion of each step).

B. Overall: duration of entire activity (proposed and actual).

An example of a work plan for an individual activity is given at right.

All activities should then be summarized on a general planning sheet for the product group concerned, indicating estimated duration and providing space for the actual figures to be filled in as implementation progresses. The summary sheet should enable the TPO to reschedule events as required.

Programme Size and Duration

Experience has shown that an average-size TPO can effectively implement a maximum of five product-oriented export promotion programmes at the same time. This presupposes, however, adequate TPO resources, the commitment of the business community and of individual manufacturers, and many other factors. It is always better to start with a limited number of programmes than to begin with more and then be obliged to cancel some of them later.

Example: Work Plan by Activity-
Product: Textile Garments for Men

Activity No. 5

Purpose: Participation in the International Ready-to-wear Garment Fair in Munich

1. *Participants*

Company	Company Representative	Telephone
....	....	....
....	....	....
....	....	....
....	....	....
....	....	....

2. *Organizations Involved in Executing the Activity*

	Name	*Title*	*Telephone*
Trade Promotion Division (TPD)	....		
	....		
	....		
Exporters Association (EA)	....		
Garment Industries Association (GIA)	....		
Embassy of the Federal Republic of Germany (EFRG)	....		
....	....		
....	....		

3 *Programme of Action*

Steps	*Institution responsible (days)*	*Estimated duration (days)*	*Actual duration*	*Remarks*
1. Estimation of participation costs; communication to participants	TPD	30		
2. Final agreement on the participants	EA/GIA	8		
3. Booking of fair facilities	TPD/EFRG	25		
4. Reception of contract; signing and mailing of the contract	TPD	15		
5. Preparation and collection of samples	EFRG/GIA/TPD	20		
6. Mailing of samples to Munich	TPD	8		
7. Etc..				
	Total:		Total:	

In general, a product-and market oriented export promotion programme must be designed for a period of three years as it is usually impossible to introduce a product into a new market and to attain a significant volume of sales before two years of continuous effort.

Costs

It is important for the TPO (and eventually the other participating organizations) to calculate the cost of each activity. It should ensure that the required provisions are made in its budget for the portion of those activities that it will finance, such as staff to manage the programmes. Each programme requires a full-time coordinator, who is usually one of the TPO's product managers, and perhaps an assistant.

These cost estimates will enable the TPO to determine to what extent the producers concened should participate financially in the programme. No services of this type should be given entirely free of charge, as this tends to weaken the participants' commitment to the programme When a company's financial participation is required, the decision to participate is taken at a higher management level than when services are free, and greater attention is paid to the quality of services received and the results attained. Knowledge of the cost per activity will also allow participants with limited resources to decide whether to participate in the programme partially or not at all.

Inter-institutional Committee

The TPO may implement product-oriented programmes largely on its own, seeking the cooperation of other entitles as and when required. Ad hoc collaboration is sometimes difficult to obtain, however, either because of a lack of interest or for bureaucratic reasons. Many countries in Europe, Latin America and Asia have therefore established inter-institutional committees, as a continuation of the preparatory working groups mentioned above, composed of all of the private and public entities concerned to ensure their active participation in implementing the marketing programmes.

Among the functions of such a committee are:

Coordinate the activities of the participating and implementing agencies.

Periodically review the progress of the programme.

Find solutions to problems that may arise and adapt programme activities accordingly.

Channel all assistance available from outside organizations, whether national or international, private or public, to the programme.

Represent the interests of producers in negotiations with public bodies to facilitate the implementation of the programme.

The committee should have respresentatives from selected companies, the TPO and all of the government organizations concerned. Some of the same institutions involved in the working groups can be asked to join this committee. The members must be chosen carefully and hold high enough positions in their respective organizations to obtain approval of recommendations without difficulty.

Company Marketing Programmes

Export promotion programmes following a product and market approach, as described above, can serve as the basis for individual marketing programmes of the companies concerned. In other words, the global product programmes can provide a framework within which the companies can design and implement their own short and medium-term marketing plans.

The global programme lists the marketing targets and the specific actions to be carried out to achieve them. Each company can select the markets of greatest interest and choose, among the various joint promotional activities, those that will be the most beneficial to it. It can also get the advise of the TPO product specialists on individual actions that will help the company to penetrate the market.

Evaluating the Programme

Continued follow up by the inter-institutional committee can be one of the best evaluation techniques for the different programmes.

At the end of each year, a balance sheet should be prepared comparing objectives with the results obtained. This annual report should also outline the activities planned for the following year. It should be widely distributed The report is important for government decisionmakers because it constitutes a record of the TPO's achievements any may result in improved political, technical and financial support from government ministries and private organizations. The annual report will enable commercial attaches abroad to focus their search for import opportunities on priority sectors or products.

If reliable trade statistics are available, it might also be possible to evaluate the programme in terms of its effect on the volume or value of exports to a given market. This evaluation cannot be made, however, until the programme has been under way for several years.